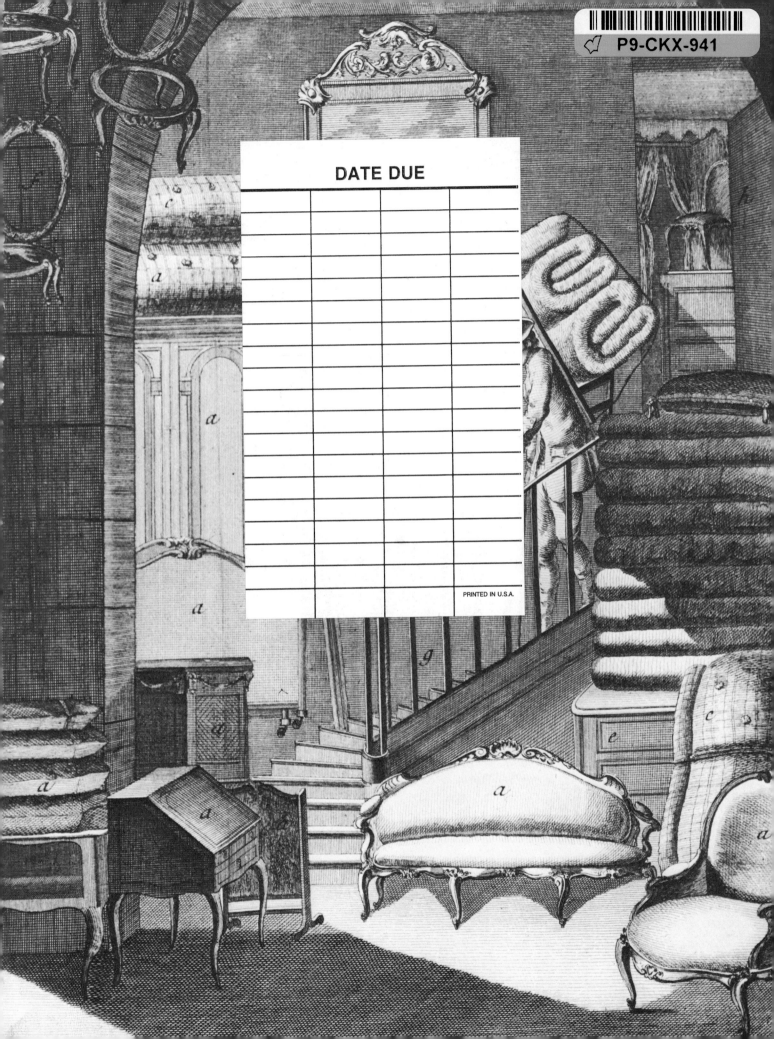

DATE DUE

Furniture 1

General Editor: Brenda Gilchrist

Furniture 1

PREHISTORIC THROUGH ROCOCO

Robert Bishop & Patricia Coblentz

COOPER-HEWITT MUSEUM

The Smithsonian Institution's National Museum of Design

ENDPAPERS

An upholstery workshop of eighteenth-century France as shown in Diderot's *Encyclopédie ou Dictionnaire raisonné des sciences, des arts et des métiers*. Published in Paris between 1751 and 1780, and comprising thirty-five volumes, the *Encyclopédie* was an extraordinary work covering the sciences, arts and trades or professions of the day, with thousands of illustrations showing how things were made. This illustration is from a volume published in 1771. Cooper-Hewitt Museum Library

FRONTISPIECE

Room designed by Nicolas Pineau for the Hôtel de Varengeville, Paris, commissioned by the Duchesse de Villars. French, c. 1735. Metropolitan Museum of Art, New York, acquired with funds given by Mr. and Mrs. Charles B. Wrightsman, 1963

Art Direction, Design: JOSEPH B. DEL VALLE

Text Editor: JOAN HOFFMAN

Picture Editor: LISA LITTLE

Contents

1 INTRODUCTION 7

2 THE ANCIENT WORLD 13

3 MEDIEVAL FORMS 27

4 THE RENAISSANCE 35

5 THE BAROQUE 49

6 ONE HUNDRED YEARS OF GREAT FURNITURE DESIGN 84

7 ADVICE FOR THE COLLECTOR 120

    Glossary 122

    Reading and Reference 123

    Some Public Collections of Furniture 124

    Index 125

    Acknowledgments/Credits 128

1 Introduction

In the history of furniture, a myriad of forms and a wealth of decorative motifs evolved. *Furniture 1: Prehistoric Through Rococo* is a concise presentation of the major developments in furniture design and use, beginning in the ancient world and continuing through the introduction of machine technology about 1800. Furniture making is discussed as a craft, and social background has been included so that the reader can understand how furniture was used in everyday life.

Furniture has a long and distinguished history, and man has drawn on a variety of materials to make his furniture. The materials most frequently used have been wood, metal and stone.

Little is known of the furniture of prehistoric man, but he probably used found objects to satisfy basic needs: a rock with a hollow could serve as a seat; one with a broad, flat surface, as a table. Later, however, as he attempted to construct furniture more closely suited to his needs, he sought materials with particular qualities—materials that could be readily worked and that were resilient and in plentiful supply. The best material available to fill all these requirements was wood. Nearly all consciously constructed prehistoric furniture was assembled with the basic *post-and-lintel* system, in which vertical uprights support a horizontal member. It was simple but effective.

Once metalworking techniques developed during the Bronze Age, craftspeople constructed furniture from various metals, such as bronze and iron. Metal, however, was more often used for decorative purposes, and wood remained the most popular structural material.

Furniture could also be fashioned from woven or braided material, including first and foremost wicker. This humble material required only the gathering of natural plant forms that could be easily woven into tables, chairs or other utilitarian objects. It is not surprising that wicker furniture was popular in the ancient world and has never passed from favor.

Colorplate 1.
Architectural cabinet-on-stand with sculptural finials and base supports. It is veneered with ebony and tortoiseshell; the drawers and doors are inset with marble panels painted with biblical scenes. Flemish, c. 1650. Rijksmuseum, Amsterdam

Countless natural plants were useful for the weaving of chair seats. The three major types have been rush, made from twisted cattails; splint, derived from thinly sliced segments of such supple trees as the ash; and cane, from bamboo, rattan or certain palm trees.

From the earliest times craftspeople strove to improve physical comfort by designing better furniture. At first, skins were stretched across seat or bed frames. Later, tanned leather replaced the simple stretched skins. An even greater luxury arose when textiles were used in combination with furniture. The wealth of a man could often be judged by the number of pieces of furniture in his home, and textiles added greatly to their worth.

From primitive times, a basic method of furniture construction has been *joinery*—a technique by which pieces are specifically shaped to fit together. *Mortise-and-tenon joints*—in which a *tenon*, or protrusion, of one piece is fitted into a *mortise*, or groove, of the other—are particularly important in joinery. *Joiners*, as specialists in joinery were called, not only built ships and houses but made furniture as well. Many collectors erroneously believe, however, that all early furniture was pegged and that screws and nails indicate either poor construction or that the pieces are of late date. This is simply untrue. Even ancient Egyptian furniture was constructed with nails, and occasionally screws were used.

Another common misconception is that the drawers in all early furniture were *dovetailed*, or united at the corners with interwoven wedge-shaped mortise-and-tenon joints. The use of dovetailing as we know it today did not become popular until the seventeenth century, when craft guilds encouraged any refinements in furniture production that would bolster the idea of specialization they so adamantly supported.

After the basic crafting of a piece of furniture, decoration was often added. It was generally one of three types: carved, painted or applied.

Carved decoration ranged from relatively easily executed incised scratch or chip carving to low-relief carving to three-dimensional carving that is often sculptural in effect.

Painted decoration can be used to achieve two goals: it can make furniture more colorful, or it can disguise the fact that a piece might have been made of inferior woods or of different woods that would take a natural finish in an uneven manner. *Gilding* (overlaying wood with a thin layer of gold leaf) and *lacquering* (decorating with colorful varnishes) also created a luxurious finish.

Surface treatment could emphasize the beauty of the wood as well; staining, varnishing, polishing and waxing were various methods of finishing a piece.

Furniture makers in all periods have always had great opportunities for embellishing their works with other materials. As elegant furniture became a symbol of the owner's social position or political power, a natural desire for decorated pieces appeared. Applied turned motifs (fashioned while the wood was revolving on a lathe), carefully wrought moldings and precious and semiprecious stones, as well as silver and gold, provided additional splendor.

Other ways of enriching furniture developed as well. *Veneer*, a thin layer of surface wood often selected for its rarity or rich grain, was bonded to a carcass usually constructed from solid woods of lesser beauty. *Marquetry*, a process by which thinly sliced materials such as wood, ivory, bone, metal or mother-of-pearl were veneered onto the surface of a piece, could be used to create decorative pictorial scenes or floral motifs. *Parquetry*, a similar technique using geometric designs, also produced a variegated decorative effect.

As we have said, from the time of the Bronze Age metals have always been an important part of furniture construction and design. Bronze, iron, silver, gold, brass and even steel were used to create entire pieces of furniture. Individual decorative or functional elements could be fashioned from these metals and applied to a body constructed from another medium. None, however, produced as sumptuous effects as the meticulously *chased* (indented with a hammer) *ormolu* (gilded bronze) decoration that was first used in France during the seventeenth century. The popularity of ormolu reached its zenith in the Parisian cabinetmaking shops during the reign of Louis XV in the mid-eighteenth century.

In the illustrations on the next two pages, the individual parts of a secretary-desk, a table and a chair have been labeled to help the reader understand some of the technical terms used throughout the text.

Because of their great age and rarity and their infrequent appearance in the marketplace, many of the individual pieces described in this volume are relatively inaccessible to today's collectors. At the end of the book we have listed the major public museums in which types of furniture similar to those illustrated can be seen, and we recommend that anyone wishing to acquire additional knowledge about world furniture prior to 1800 visit some of these institutions.

Since authentic furniture crafted before 1800 is somewhat scarce, collectors may want to consider pieces from the various revival styles popular during the nineteenth and early twentieth centuries to re-create in spirit, if not in actuality, the period of their interest.

Our final chapter contains special information that will serve as a guide to future collectors. Collecting furniture can be a rewarding experience, for learning about the past through the actual furnishings used by our predecessors imparts a special knowledge that can be acquired in no other way.

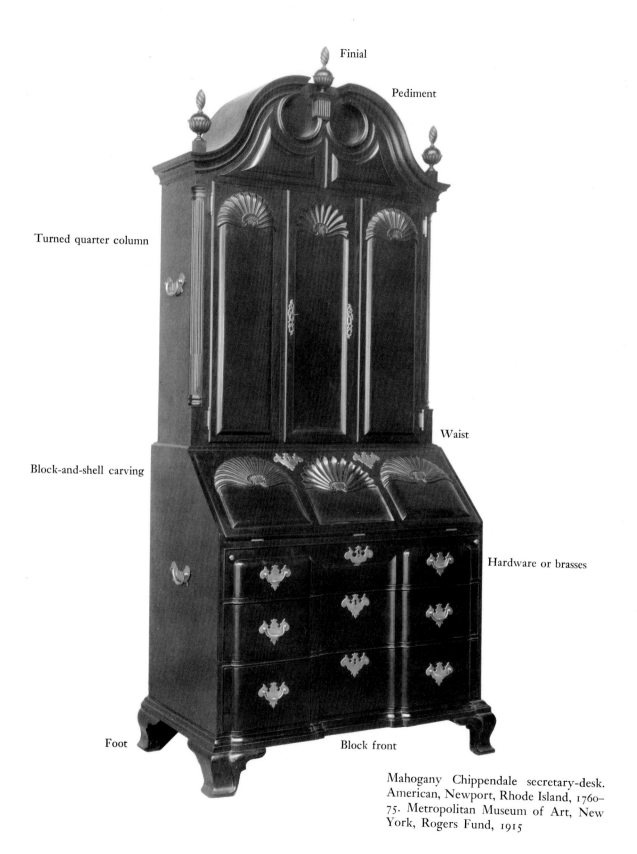

Finial

Pediment

Turned quarter column

Waist

Block-and-shell carving

Hardware or brasses

Foot

Block front

Mahogany Chippendale secretary-desk. American, Newport, Rhode Island, 1760–75. Metropolitan Museum of Art, New York, Rogers Fund, 1915

Crest rail

Stile

Splat

Side rail or seat rail

Apron or skirt

Cabriole leg

Claw-and-ball foot

Mahogany Chippendale side chair. American, Philadelphia, 1760–80. Collections of Greenfield Village and the Henry Ford Museum, Dearborn, Mich.

Top

Drop leaf

Drawer

Swinging gate support

Leg

Stretcher

Foot

Mahogany gateleg table. American, New England, 1695–1720. From Collections of Greenfield Village and the Henry Ford Museum, Dearborn, Mich.

2   The Ancient World

The history of furniture begins in prehistoric times, when men and women living in simple shelters introduced various elements to make life easier and more comfortable and to fill their practical needs. Seats and sleeping pallets and other sorts of rudimentary furniture were probably made out of objects they found around them, such as rocks and branches from trees.

In time, wide-ranging nomadic tribes curtailed the extent of their migrations. A seminomadic existence led man to construct more permanent domiciles and to hollow out from trees such basic furniture as the box or trunk, which could be used not only for storage but for sitting. Chairs were relatively few and were usually reserved for religious or political leaders. However, benches, stools and even hammocks were in general use. The elaborate hairstyles worn by the upper classes gave rise to special-purpose pieces such as the neckrest and headrest.

As man became more settled, and tightly knit social groups with structured religious and political concerns evolved in the Mediterranean, the importance of family and community life grew too. Dwellings became permanent, and furniture proliferated in both form and quantity.

In ancient Egypt, homes of the important personages were richly decorated, although they were sparsely furnished by today's standards. The excavations of Egyptian tombs have enabled historians to learn about Egyptian life through the paintings on walls and on artifacts. At the same time, they have provided actual examples of the incredibly lavish furniture associated with the ruling upper classes, for the Egyptian attempted to re-create his life in the hereafter just as it had been while he was living on earth. Food, clothing and the furniture necessary for sustenance and comfort after burial were often included in the tomb with the deceased. From both paintings and surviving pieces it is thus possible to reconstruct the upper-class

Colorplate 2.
Ceremonial chair from the tomb of Tutankhamun. Made of wood with ivory, sheet gold overlay and bronze, it was probably used as his coronation chair. The kneeling figure represents Heh, the god of eternity. Egyptian, c. 1334–1325 B.C. Egyptian Museum, Cairo

Egyptian home, the arrangement of rooms and the furniture in them.

Furniture from the Old Kingdom (c. 2700–2200 B.C.) possessed a quiet dignity and strength deriving from its simplicity. Furniture from this period has not survived in large enough amounts to study; however, from viewing wall paintings one can deduce that most free-standing furniture of the Old Kingdom can be placed in two distinct categories: platforms, which included benches, chairs, tables, beds, couches and stools (plate 1); and boxes, the basic form for chests and cupboards.

Surface ornament consisted of carved decoration or gilding. However, many pieces depended upon their shape, proportion and texture for effect. Thrones and chairs, symbols of honor or power, were carved with lion-paw feet; beds were ornamented with animal skins and lively, decorated mats. All these point to the Egyptian concern with decoration as well as comfort. Stools, footrests, chests, small cabinets, small tables and even vase stands were an indication of highly organized living patterns. Especially popular were four-legged stools with animal-shaped legs and square seats made from concave wood or woven or braided rushes. Chairs with arms and

1.
Stela made of painted limestone showing a stool with animal-form legs and feet and a simple table that is supported on a wall bracket. Egyptian, 2570–2450 B.C. Lowie Museum of Anthropology, University of California, Berkeley

Colorplate 3.
Wooden chest from the tomb of Tutankhamun. It has a gesso surface and inset panels of carved and painted ivory and is decorated with scenes showing the king and his queen. Egyptian, c. 1334–1325 B.C. Egyptian Museum, Cairo

backs began to appear during the second half of the Old Kingdom. Large tables were relatively rare. Egyptians were adept in the use of base metals and often incorporated them into furniture designs. Decoration in the form of *inlay* (a process whereby contrasting materials are set into the surface of a piece), relief carvings and gilding increased. Rich fabrics were often used as accessories.

During the Middle Kingdom (c. 2065–1785 B.C.), a growing sophistication evolved, and embellishments such as paint, gilt, veneer and inlay became an integral part of all furniture design. Representations of lion heads, cow heads and hippopotamuses (sacred animals) were popular design motifs.

The love of luxury increased during the Empire, or New Kingdom (c. 1570–1085 B.C.), and in cities such as Thebes, the capital, magnificent palaces, tombs and temples were constructed on both

2.
Headrest for use on a bed. From the tomb of the pharaoh Tutankhamun. Made of ivory, with a wooden dowel and gold nails. Egyptian, c. 1334–1325 B.C. Egyptian Museum, Cairo

sides of the Nile. Lavishly decorated furniture, like that preserved in the tombs of the pharaohs, was produced on a grand scale. Construction of Egyptian furniture during this time was highly sophisticated.

It seems fairly certain that the Egyptians invented the lathe and the mortise-and-tenon joint. Tomb paintings dating from c. 1380 B.C. indicate that craftsmen enjoyed well-equipped workshops, where the arts of joinery, turning and cabinetmaking had been carried on since remote Egyptian history. Turnings on the legs of Egyptian stools and chairs were complex, and craftsmen appear to have favored a concave outline extensively decorated with rings.

During the Empire, Egypt extended her borders through conquests from Nubia to the Euphrates. Her increased contact with foreign countries brought new design ideas and new furniture forms to the tradition-bound country. In well-to-do homes chairs became more plentiful. Folding stools, regarded as symbols of authority, were frequently painted in brilliant colors. Small, low tables, often woven from rush, were used where easily movable furniture was desired. Beds consisted of a wooden frame with or without legs. Skin or cloth, or occasionally braided natural fibers or strips of leather, was stretched over the frame. Most frequently, beds stood on wooden or ivory legs often terminating in the shape of animal hooves. Elaborate pieces, such as gaming boards supported on carved legs, were popular.

In 1922, in one of modern archaeology's most exciting finds, some of Egypt's most celebrated furniture was discovered in the unrifled Empire tomb of the young king Tutankhamun (reigned c. 1334–1325 B.C.). The meticulously designed pieces of unprecedented magnificence reflect his enormous wealth. Beautifully constructed wooden chairs (colorplate 2) and couches were ornamented with open relief carvings and precious metal inlays and overlays. Ivory headrests were embellished with three-dimensional carvings (plate 2). Small chests (colorplate 3) used in life for writing materials and the storage of household linens and clothing were also superbly decorated. The dry climate of Egypt has preserved an astonishing amount of furniture, allowing us today to study centuries-old pieces.

The Egyptians were skillful metalworkers and developed metal casting to a high degree. Fragments indicate that metalsmithing was also familiar to the inhabitants of the Mesopotamian Valley. Bronze was occasionally used on furniture in Babylonia, but more frequently metalsmiths cast copper or hammered it into thin plates for decorative inlays and freestanding sculptural embellishments for furniture.

In the Assyrian Empire, which flourished between 1200 B.C. and 612 B.C., large complex palaces were decorated with bold vigorous sculptures in the form of winged, animal-pawed, human-bodied monsters. Furniture illustrated in stone friezes, such as one depicting

King Ashur-bani-pal (reigned 669–626 B.C.) feasting with his queen (plate 3), indicates that the Assyrians were adept at the use of the lathe. The couch, the chair, the footstool and the table between them all have conelike, turned legs typical of this era.

In early Greece, houses, even of the well-to-do, were considered primarily as places in which to retire in the evening. Consequently, rooms were not numerous, nor were they more than sparsely furnished.

Since few actual pieces of Greek furniture remain, one must turn to sources such as vase painting to learn about the forms. From these secondary sources we find that the *diphros* (a simple stool with X-shaped legs) was probably the oldest and most frequently used seating piece in all of Greece (plate 4). The also popular *diphros okladias* (folding stool), of Egyptian derivation and most common during the sixth and fifth centuries B.C., had two sets of crossed legs fastened with a bolt at the crossing and frequently ending in animal-paw feet. The *bathron* (a box-type stool or bench) had its prototype in stone and was usually fitted with cushions. The *thronos* (throne) was, of course, the most sumptuous type of furniture used for seating and often was ornately decorated and further embellished with precious stones. A *threnys* (footstool) was nearly always used in conjunction with a throne and sometimes with other seating pieces as well.

The most typical furniture of ancient Greece was created between the seventh and fourth centuries B.C., and the most successful balance between tradition and function occurred during the fifth century B.C. It is at this time that a notable furniture type, the *klismos* (plate 5), is found. This chair, used frequently in the home, perfectly satisfied its function and, at the same time, combined simplicity and extreme

3.
Stone frieze carved with a scene of King Ashur-bani-pal feasting with his queen. The king reclines on a high couch furnished with a mattress and bolster, which would probably also serve as a throne. The queen sits on a thronelike armchair with her feet on a footstool. Assyrian, c. 669–626 B.C. British Museum, London

4

5

4.
Attic white-ground pyxis, painted with a scene of a Muse seated on an X stool, or *diphros*, playing a lyre. Greek, 460–450 B.C. Museum of Fine Arts, Boston, H. L. Pierce Fund

5.
The painting on this red-figured lekythos illustrates a *klismos* chair, which has concave legs in the front and rear that splay outward. The back consists of a shallow concave backrest, providing comfort for the sitter. Greek, 450–440 B.C. Metropolitan Museum of Art, New York, Rogers Fund, 1915

elegance. The *stiles* (vertical pieces) of the back splayed outward, and the concave backrest supported the sitter at shoulder height. It almost never had arms. The front and back legs were formed of concave opposed curves, thus giving a sense of resiliency to the delicate form. The *klismos* was almost always made of wood and frequently was devoid of applied decoration, relying upon simple lines for its beauty. It is not surprising that the *klismos* form was revived during the Middle Ages and again at the opening of the nineteenth century, when pieces recalling ancient lifestyles were especially popular.

In addition to the *klismos*, the bed or couch was another type of Greek furniture to develop a peculiar characteristic form. Sometime near the beginning of the sixth century B.C., it became customary for

6.
Guests at a Greek banquet enjoy music and wine. They are reclining on the couches (*klines*) that at night were also used as beds for sleeping. Drawn after a painted scene on a Greek kylix dating from 510 B.C., now in the British Museum, London

7.
Bronze chair from Chiusi. It is decorated with raised geometric patterns. Etruscan, seventh–fourth century B.C. University Museum, Philadelphia

8.
Bronze lamp holder, or *thymiaterion*. These devices provided illumination for Etruscan and Roman houses. Etruscan, seventh–fourth century B.C. Lowie Museum of Anthropology, University of California, Berkeley

6

Greeks to eat in a reclining position. The *kline* (plate 6), a couch used for both sleeping and dining, became therefore the most important piece of furniture in the household. It, too, reached its finest degree of development in the fifth century B.C., when banquets and other social gatherings called for more elaborate homes with rooms explicitly reserved for dining.

Small, light, portable tables that could be easily stored were brought out when required at mealtime to hold the abundant repast. Between the sixth and fourth centuries B.C., the *tripous*, or three-legged tripod table, was developed, and a rectangular table with four legs, for use as a worktable in the home and by craftsmen in the shops, became popular. Although the round table with a single central support or pedestal had been developed in Egypt, it was not so popular in Greece as was the round table with three legs, an indigenous Greek invention.

Chests, though rarely surviving today, were known in obscure Greek antiquity. Most were made of wood; others found on Crete were shaped from terra cotta. These were fitted with simple feet and

7

had a peaked cover. During the classical period (in the fifth century B.C.) the box or chest underwent a dramatic change and became a rectangular container with a flat lid. Greater attention was paid to its design, construction and decoration, and it developed into a refined piece of cabinetmaking.

Cupboards for storage, more utilitarian than the chest, were especially popular in the Hellenistic period (c. 400–first century B.C.). During this period, furniture assumed an important place in the decorative scheme of the home. New forms were created, but the three basic seating pieces—the stool, the chair and the throne—continued to be the most frequently used furniture. Furniture was embellished with simple painted and inlaid decorations that became an integral part of the overall design. Popular motifs were palmettes and other ornaments derived from natural forms.

Greek furniture served as a prototype for peoples of the entire Mediterranean world, including the Etruscans, who during the sixth century B.C. began to borrow freely from the Greeks and integrated imported furniture designs within existing traditions. Etruscan pieces from this period tend to be crude, massive and cumbersome, indicating a failure to understand Greek concepts of design fully. Although the Etruscans furnished their homes in a fashion similar to that of the Greeks, very little Etruscan furniture is comparable in beauty to the Greek prototypes it attempted to mimic. However, costly Etruscan seating pieces of wood or stone were often embellished with applied metal decoration. Metal was also cast in the form of benches, chairs (plate 7) and lighting devices such as the *thymiaterion* (plate 8). The Etruscans shared the Greek custom of reclining while eating; a popular form therefore was the couch, supported upon rectangular or turned legs. Like the Greeks, the Etruscans were fond of beautiful textiles, and one can assume that couches were made comfortable and luxurious by the addition of cushions and pillows.

Etruscan and Roman furniture is best viewed as a synthesis of foreign influences and already well-established indigenous Italian forms. Rome, as the center of world power, brought together all earlier Mediterranean cultures and is often regarded as the basic symbol of the art of antiquity. Greek furniture design was, of course, a major part of Rome's inheritance from the past.

By the third century B.C., Roman chests, chairs and beds assumed a distinctive style. The well-to-do Roman homeowner clearly revealed his love of luxury. Furniture had two important functions—to accommodate the practical needs of the owner and to express his taste and status.

Roman craftsmen fashioned beautiful furniture that was held in high esteem. The perfection of metalworking techniques enabled artisans to achieve a new plasticity in their cast-metal pieces.

8

About the second century B.C., bronze couches laden with inlay became important furnishings in the stylish home. A modest version of the Greek couch continued to be popular in the Roman household. In time, decorative elements in the form of animal and human figures appeared (plate 9).

Romans had a predilection for tables with four legs, and inventive craftsmen developed a variety of sizes for a multitude of uses. Table legs were frequently sculptural, and animal forms were especially favored. Plant motifs also abounded on Roman tables, which in many instances were fitted with elegant polished marble tops.

The Greek *klismos* served as an immediate predecessor of the *cathedra*, a favorite chair with Roman women (plate 10). Stools, too, were popular, and the folding stool, or *sella curulis*, was much in demand by senators and magistrates. The *solium*, or seat of honor, was similar to the Greek throne and was often used in the atrium by the head of the family when receiving honored guests or clients. A carved mourning scene on a second-century A.D. sarcophagus (plate 11) shows several pieces of Roman furniture, including a couch, a chair and a stool.

The *armarium* (cupboard) was most frequently constructed of wood and on occasion embellished with inlay of rare and beautiful woods or ivory. It was generally fitted with two doors that had *openwork* (decorative perforations) in the upper panels, thus provid-

9.
Ivory couch decorated with bone carvings and glass inlay. The lion heads and carved busts are typical details. Roman, first century A.D. Metropolitan Museum of Art, New York, gift of J. Pierpont Morgan, 1917

10.
Wall painting from a villa at Boscoreale showing a lady playing the cithara. She is seated in a thronelike chair, or *cathedra*. Roman, first century B.C. Metropolitan Museum of Art, New York, Rogers Fund, 1903

ing for the circulation of air. Folding doors were also known to the Romans, who used them on medium-size cupboards.

Chests, for the most part, continued to be crude. They were often covered with sheets of metal and bolted to the floor so that they might also serve as safes. This use may partly explain the lack of refinement in the massive pieces.

Classical furniture types that had evolved earlier continued to be in fashion in Rome about A.D. 200. Furniture varied according to the wealth and social position of the homeowner. The poor and the large slave population possessed little of their own.

In the fourth century, two related events altered the history of the world. First, under Constantine I (306–337) Christianity was recognized as the official religion of the Roman state. Second, before the close of Constantine's reign, the capital of his empire was moved from Rome to Byzantium, which was rebuilt and renamed Constantinople. This move resulted in the ultimate division of the Roman Empire into two distinct parts, the Western and Eastern empires.

In Europe successive waves of barbarian invaders infiltrated what had been the cultured world. Since the barbarians were essentially nomadic, their primary artistic endeavors were in the form of metal weapons and objects of personal adornment. Refinements such as well-crafted furniture became less important. In time furniture was reduced to pieces that were easily transportable, and only items such as folding stools remained popular. Since the nomadic conquerors brought with them no furniture-making traditions, they adopted the furniture forms of the countries they conquered.

Along with these major political shifts and the resulting social turmoil came a serious alteration in the standard of living for the population of the Roman Empire. Social upheaval typically results in a decline in the need for the craftsman's products, and thus in craftsmanship as well. Though this was the situation in the West, the classical forms and techniques did survive in the furniture of Byzantium (the Eastern Roman Empire).

In Byzantium few structural changes in furniture developed; most changes occurred in decoration. Enamel plaques, applied metal decorations wrought from silver and gold and embellishments of mother-of-pearl inlay and veneer were added to make pieces such as the *cathedra* even more luxurious. Modest furniture was enriched by low-relief surface carving.

Thrones continued to be symbols of authority, and the footrests of the earlier period developed into podiums often encrusted with precious metals in decorative geometric forms. Such pieces, which were not movable, were often made even more important by the addition of an architectural canopy. Since the church became a major patron of furniture makers, many of the noteworthy pieces of furniture from this period were made for ecclesiastical purposes.

The Byzantines favored the *kline* as a seating form to be used along with a table until the end of the eleventh century. Then it began to fade from popularity, supplanted by three-legged seating pieces with semicircular backs and by more modest benches and stools. The shapes of tables proliferated—rectangular, square, semicircular and round—and were partly determined by the use for which the piece was intended. Monumental tables were especially popular at banquets and other special court functions, and even small round tables were lavishly encrusted with precious inlays.

Chests continued to be one of the most frequently used articles of household furniture, and their degree of sophistication depended entirely upon the household for which they were made. Jeweled, inlaid examples, often of large size, were the repository for precious goods and coveted textiles. Smaller caskets or jewel boxes, often worked of wood or ivory, were decorated with zoomorphic designs identical to those found on chests.

In the homes of the elite, rooms set aside especially for sleeping provided unprecedented comfort. These sleeping rooms usually contained a four-legged bed that was so high it could only be reached by steps. Textiles used on the bed were among the most expensive of the household furnishings. Simple beds, generally pallets laid upon the floor, were the fare of most, although some people of modest means slept on cots.

The use of rooms for specific purposes increased. Men of learning took great delight in establishing a workroom that served as a study. Rudimentary writing tables, small writing stands on legs, tables fitted with lecterns and center tables fitted with doors and shelves to hold writing implements became especially popular in a society that appreciated literacy and maintained respect for education. Small cupboards were designed for the exclusive storage of treasured books. Studies were furnished in a relatively simple manner appropriate to monastic life, whereas court furniture increased in sumptuousness and monumental scale.

11.
Sarcophagus carved with a mourning scene for a young girl. This piece illustrates a thronelike chair, a couch on turned legs and a folding stool with X-shaped legs. Roman, second century A.D. British Museum, London

Colorplate 4.
The center and right panels from the Merode Altarpiece showing details of the interiors and furnishings of a medieval house. In the center panel is a bench with carved Gothic designs under the seat and a table with a top that tilts and can be placed upright against the wall. In the right panel is a high-backed settle and a simple table of plank construction. The altarpiece was painted by Robert Campin, who was active by 1406 and died in 1444. Flemish, early fifteenth century. Detail. Metropolitan Museum of Art, New York, Cloisters Collection

3 Medieval Forms

The term Middle Ages refers to the period between A.D. 476, when Romulus Augustulus, the last emperor of the Western Roman Empire, was deposed, and A.D. 1453, when Constantinople was conquered by the Turks.

Within this enormous length of time, Western society underwent great changes, including the dissolution of organized government on a large scale. However, under the brilliant leadership of Charlemagne (king of the Franks 768–814; emperor of the West 800–814), the Carolingian dynasty reorganized Western society by bringing order from chaos and, in spite of the fluctuating reins of power in Europe, provided an impetus for the survival of classical learning. The furniture of the Carolingian period, which lasted until 911 in Germany and 987 in France, reveals this impressive survival.

Carolingian dwellings, for the most part, were stark and without refinement. Furniture was based upon Roman prototypes, and nearly every household, from the palace to the most modest hut, contained benches and three-legged stools. The folding stool carried with it the connotation of power, as it had done in the ancient world, and it was still used by both religious and political authorities. Comfort, however, was a minor concern, and cushions, pads and other ease-giving objects were not in so much demand as they had been with the luxury-loving Romans. Although wood appears to have been the primary material for furniture construction, bronze pieces were occasionally fashioned.

Large stationary tables, both round and rectangular, appeared. Legs on substantial pieces were nearly always sculptural and based on animal forms inherited from the Greeks and Romans. Rectangular tables, often constructed so that they could be easily disassembled and set up only for special purposes such as dining, frequently consisted of a board placed on top of X-shaped legs or sawhorselike supports. A fifteenth-century example is shown in plate 12.

As in earlier periods, the bed continued to be the most important piece of furniture in any household because it could be hung with

12.
Detail of a page from an illuminated manuscript depicting Charles the Bold (1433–1477) presiding at a meeting of the Order of the Golden Fleece. He sits on a canopied throne that appears to be covered with a textile. In the foreground is a table consisting of a board placed on top of sawhorselike supports. French, c. 1473. Österreichische National-bibliothek, Vienna

precious textiles indicating the wealth of the owner. These draperies also provided privacy and protected sleepers against the cold in drafty rooms. Beds of this period were fashioned with turned headposts and footposts and often stood on high legs.

Studies, or libraries, remained popular among the upper classes; however, the furnishings changed. Writing accouterments—pens, inks and sanders—were stored in rectangular chests with tops that could be lifted, such as the late fifteenth-century example illustrated in plate 13. It seems reasonable to assume that large chests, sometimes mounted on feet, were also used for the storage of clothing and other prized fabrics. The lectern was popular and often was supported on a high pedestal, which in turn rested upon a tripodlike base. These pieces could serve as writing desks as well.

Much of the information about furniture between the fall of the Roman Empire and the opening of the Romanesque period in the eleventh century is derived from secondary sources—paintings, decorative carving on sculpture and illuminated manuscripts. Although few actual examples remain, surviving pieces from the mid-eleventh century on do enable us to establish a clear picture of lifestyles and furniture design.

During the Romanesque period, which extended through the twelfth century, architecture and furniture indicated a steadily growing social stability. Because this period was dominated by military exploits, invasions and paralyzing feudalism, the principal stimulus for the creation of art and furniture emanated from the monasteries. The most important buildings were churches, and ecclesiastical furniture was made by local craftsmen in native styles. Decorative embellishments, however, were a mingling of naturalistic forms from the West and stylized geometric abstractions from the East. Furniture created out of parts shaped on a rudimentary lathe or great wheel, as in ancient Egypt, reappeared during the late twelfth and thirteenth centuries.

Storage chests similar in design to ancient sarcophagi and wooden coffins became especially popular. Decoration took many forms. Some pieces were carved, some were embellished with painted parchment or fine linen and some with applied ornamentation in the form of rosettes or architectural motifs.

Folding stools remained popular with the upper classes, but their use now extended to the middle classes as well.

During the decline of the Romanesque period and the emergence of the Gothic period, which extended from the twelfth through the sixteenth century, feudalism continued. However, in contrast to the anarchy of the earlier Romanesque period, it was an ordered feudalism. By the thirteenth century centralized governments were established in both England and France, and confidence in the future replaced the blind insecurity of the early Middle Ages.

By the thirteenth century, too, nearly every craftsman belonged to a guild. Each well-known furniture maker maintained his own shop, where boys were committed to apprenticeship between the ages of ten and twelve. An apprentice learned the fundamentals of the craft during his first few years of service and eventually was initiated into the more intricate secrets of the trade. Upon leaving his master's shop, the youth usually spent several years working in various cities as a journeyman, during which time he learned additional techniques by observing other masters. In time he became eligible for membership in the guild and thus acquired the right to establish his own shop.

The guild awarded commissions and was responsible for inspecting the quality of the materials used and the workmanship. It also received payment for its members. The guild system promoted fine craftsmanship, and under its guidance superior products were made available to the purchaser.

The Gothic cathedral with its rib vaulting, flying buttresses and brilliant glass windows was the supreme triumph of the Gothic artist. The cathedrals, however, were essentially stone and masonry skeletons that held walls of stained glass, the hallmark of the Gothic style. The mammoth arches, pillars and gigantic buttresses were embellished with large-scale carved motifs. When these motifs were used on monumental freestanding pieces of wooden furniture in the church proper, such as altar screens and other ritual furnishings, they retained their strong visual impact. On the other hand, when the decorative schemes were applied to furniture in the home, they often lost much of their strength because of the reduction in scale.

Furniture construction changed during the Gothic period, and skeletonlike frames were united by inserted decorative panels that served the same function as did the walls of glass in the cathedral. The earlier plank construction of the Romanesque period was replaced by framed panels consisting of vertical and horizontal members today known as *stiles* and *rails*, respectively. The mortise-and-tenon joint, first developed by the Egyptians, was reintroduced, and furniture became lighter, stronger and more permanent. The basic decorative motifs of Gothic design used on furniture are the *pointed arch*, the *quatrefoil* (four-petaled flower or leaf), the *trefoil* (three-petaled flower or leaf) and, slightly later, the carved *linenfold* panel (sometimes referred to as *parchment* panel, decorated with a representation of a scroll of linen).

The rise of universities in the Gothic period resulted in many new freedoms. Secular arts began to replace monastic ones. The upper and middle classes became more populous, and furniture was once again in great demand, becoming more refined in both design and execution.

Some chests were decorated with incised ornament; others were embellished with the carved raised linenfolds so typical of the Gothic

13.
Oak desk with hinged top. Writing materials and books were stored inside. English, late fifteenth century. Victoria and Albert Museum, London

period. The linenfold design appeared first in Flanders, and regional variations developed soon after in England, France and Germany. Other chests were painted, and decorative metalwork provided additional strength.

Native woods were the standard fare. In the Alpine areas and in southern Germany, beech and coniferous woods were the most popular, with linden and walnut favored for carved decoration. In England, northern France, northern Germany and the Low Countries, oak and walnut were most often used. Oak was perfectly suited for situations where strong joinery was desirable.

New furniture forms evolved slowly, with some pieces designed for special purposes. In southern Germany, Italy and other areas where commerce was an important part of the economy, the counting table was especially popular.

During the Middle Ages the term *table* referred only to the top. The *frame* indicated the legs and rails, and the complete piece of furniture was known as a *table and frame*. For the most part, dining tables continued to be space savers in that they were disassembled when not in use. The term *set the table* originally referred to the process of assembling the table for a meal.

Tilt-top tables were specially constructed so that the top would tilt (colorplate 4), and the entire piece could be stored flat against the wall.

Beds were architectural in nature during the Gothic period and in many instances had high headboards topped by wooden canopies, or *testers*, decorated with carved cusped arches. The testers were draped with lavish curtains and other textiles. Iron founders sometimes were commissioned to execute beds, for in a period when vermin were especially prevalent, it was thought that metal bedsteads would prevent infestation.

Other bedroom furniture included a simple stand for a washbasin and a monumental high-backed chair with a decoratively carved canopy that served as a chair of state, from which the owner conducted his daily business and received guests. Specialized forms also developed; for example, in the fourteenth century the *prie-dieu*, or prayer table, became popular for use in the bedroom for private devotional meditation.

Easily transportable furniture continued to be important. Crusaders marched to the Holy Land, attempting to wrest it from the Muslims. At the same time devout believers made pilgrimages to churches and shrines that contained venerated relics of early religious leaders. Under these difficult nomadic conditions, a chair with back and arms was generally regarded as a royal prerogative. Folding chairs set upon a throne-like structure combining a canopy and dais became the official courts of many rulers while traveling.

Coffer makers' chairs with X-shaped frames covered with leather and studded with nails were not unlike early Roman and Egyptian X-frame stools. The leather was occasionally stamped and embossed with delicate patterns; sometimes it was even painted and gilded. When they were constructed so that they would fold, these chairs were especially popular with travelers; they were probably the progenitors of the modern director's chair.

Though thrones and grand chairs of state were handsomely designed and lavishly decorated, few of them provided the comfort of the woven (*wanded*) or basketwork pieces often used in humble peasant houses. Turned chairs with woven rush or splint seats increased in complexity, size and number. Simple versions remained popular for many centuries.

The *backstool*, a chair without arms, probably developed because of a desire to make the stool more comfortable. This was achieved by upholstering the seat and adding an upholstered back.

Settles, which were benches with high or low backs, had their origin in the fixed pews in churches but were moved out into the center of the room and became freestanding (see plate 12 and colorplate 4).

Throughout the Middle Ages chests remained important storage units in the home, and the form developed into several distinct types. The wardrobe may have evolved from the practice of setting chests one on top of another for more compact storage. Early chests nearly always had handles, but as the practice of stacking them became more widespread, the handles began to disappear; access to the stacked chests was through doors cut in the fronts rather than through the lift-tops.

The wardrobe probably made its first appearance in sacristies, where precious cloth vestments required protection. For such use the wardrobe was richly carved and painted. Wardrobes were also popular in homes, where more modest versions were commonplace.

The *plate cupboard* (literally "cup boards") developed from a single chest mounted on high legs (plate 14). It had many variants and a diversity of uses. Open-shelved cupboards (colorplate 5) designed to hold the family plate became increasingly popular. As walled cities with protective forces provided increased security, personal treasures, which had once been hidden away, could now be brought out and freely displayed.

Spanish furniture during the Middle Ages was closely related to Islamic prototypes. Exquisitely wrought metals, inlays, carving and painting were employed on a variety of simply constructed forms. Furniture consisted primarily of marriage chests, wardrobes and the seating pieces similar to those found throughout the rest of Europe during the same period. Some wardrobes had drawers behind highly

Colorplate 5 (overleaf).
Page from an illuminated manuscript illustrating an early interior. Depicted at the right is a high-backed seat of state, or throne, standing on a dais, with a carved canopy suspended above. Beyond the dais is a buffet, or plate cupboard, that is being used for the display of both utilitarian and decorative vessels. At the left several guests are seated on a bench. A luxurious fabric hanging is suspended on the wall behind them. The medieval notion of luxury demanded rich textiles; furniture decoration was of little consequence. Flemish, c. 1470–80. Reproduced from a manuscript of **Quintus Curtius** in the Bodleian Library, Oxford

lexandre
fist sumptu
eusement
mettre en
sepulture
les gens de guerre quil auoit
perdu en chassant le roy daire
et distribua .xiiii.m maretz

aux aultres compaignons
de son armee dont la pluspart
des cheuaulx fut perdue · et
mesmes ceulx qui demoure
rent pour la payne et grant
chaleur se morfondirent ·
Toute la proune quon auoit
deuant assamblee de la cite

decorated doors that were painted in a style not unlike that on Italian chests. The Spanish upper classes had to import furniture from the Low Countries since native craftsmen disregarded the new styles and continued to use traditional designs.

The Gothic period extended through the sixteenth century in some areas. Wars, famines and poor administration on the part of political rulers decimated the population and caused the joyous faith of the twelfth century to fade before a new disillusionment. At the same time, in striking contrast, the upper classes feverishly pursued pleasure through lavish pageants, festivals and feasts requiring new and elegant furniture.

Craftsmen wishing to add additional luster to their furniture occasionally applied gold leaf to various parts; such gilding was used to great effect, for it could lighten the appearance of massive pieces. Throughout the period the gilder was also trained as a painter and was called on to embellish pieces of furniture with painted decoration. One traveler reported that in the early 1500s nearly every Venetian house of the best type was furnished with bedsteads "of gold colour."

A Bohemian noble visiting Italy in 1465–66 was spellbound by the magnificent beds he saw everywhere, and he observed in the home of a Venetian merchant a piece "covered with cloth of silver and [upon it] were placed two cushions with a pillow ornamented with pearls and precious stones."

With the notable exception of Spain, most western European countries relied upon Gothic concepts of design throughout the entire fifteenth century. Gothic traditions survived in France and the Low Countries well into the sixteenth century. Toward the end of that century, Renaissance ideas and designs filtered down from their source in Italy to the rest of Europe and eventually replaced many local medieval traditions.

Collectors today have little opportunity to purchase authentic medieval furniture, since the few pieces that have survived were acquired by antiquarians during the eighteenth and nineteenth centuries and have subsequently found their way into major museum collections. Reproductions of medieval forms, however, frequently reach the marketplace, and these provide modern-day collectors with the opportunity of re-creating the feeling of a medieval interior if not the real thing.

14.
Late fifteenth-century plate cupboard with carved Gothic details on the back and the overhanging canopy. Drawn by Henry Shaw from an illuminated manuscript in the Library of the Dukes of Burgundy, Brussels, and published in his *Specimens of Ancient Furniture*, London, 1866. Cooper-Hewitt Museum Library

4   The Renaissance

The Renaissance began in Florence in the middle of the fourteenth century and continued on until the end of the sixteenth, spreading from Italy to the rest of Europe. Marking a distinct break from the Middle Ages, the Renaissance era revived the art of antiquity and generated a new spirit of humanity.

Architects such as Leon Battista Alberti (1404–1472) and Michelozzo di Bartolommeo (1396–1472) were especially influential in encouraging and fostering the Renaissance style, for they studied ancient architectural design and published their findings in such works as Alberti's *Ten Books of Architecture*. Architecture took on a new importance through these publications, which brought to popular attention the achievements of earlier cultures.

Alberti and Michelozzo executed great private palaces that mirrored the design and furnishings of sumptuous civil and religious buildings of early Rome. These magnificent Renaissance dwellings demonstrated the wealth and social position of their owners.

Along with the classically oriented and refined style of architecture, distinct new furniture styles evolved. Imposing large-scale pieces were required to fill the impressive and spacious rooms of the *palazzi*, which, however, would have still appeared sparsely furnished by our modern taste. The bedroom was a center of daily life; it served not only as a place for retiring but also as a reception area. Beds, separate and freestanding units, were fitted with tall posts and elegant canopies hung with precious fabrics, which added to their aura of importance and grandeur. *Cassoni*, or chests, were frequently used at the foot and sides of the bed, providing needed storage space, seats for visitors and steps to reach the bed, which was often inordinately high.

During the Renaissance the *cassone* developed from a simple, iron-bound chest into an elaborate, carved, painted and decorated piece of furniture (plates 15–18 and colorplate 7). It was in essence an archaic

Colorplate 6.
Two-part walnut cupboard executed in the French Renaissance style. The designs of both Du Cerceau and Sambin were undoubtedly the inspiration for the decorative carving. French, Burgundian school, sixteenth century. Philadelphia Museum of Art, purchased by Chester W. Larner

15.
Walnut *cassone* in classical sarcophagus shape. Renaissance ornament was derived from ancient Greek and Roman prototypes. This piece is decorated with entwined flowers, classical urns and griffins and has a coat of arms in the center. Italian, late fifteenth century. Victoria and Albert Museum, London

16.
Seventeenth-century design for a Renaissance-style *cassone* by an unidentified artist. Northern Italian, 1600–1650. Cooper-Hewitt Museum

form blended with a contemporary style of decoration, which sometimes included applied stucco motifs. Rich gilding, complex moldings and painted panels executed by members of the guild of *cassone* painters created an unprecedented sense of luxury. Italy had long been known for its production of splendid chests, and in 1384 Francesco Datini ordered from Florence several pieces that he wished to sell in Avignon. He requested them to be "handsome and showy and of good workmanship . . . spend on them seven or eight florins a pair; the finer and better they are, the better I can sell them." Florence remained a principal center for the manufacture of *cassoni*, and in the first half of the fifteenth century there were some ten workshops in Florence specializing in their creation.

Cradles first appeared during the Gothic period but did not become important pieces until the early fifteenth century. In 1403 Margaret of Flanders purchased two cradles for her child—a relatively simple piece for daily use and an elaborate one called a "cradell of Estate"

Colorplate 7.
Walnut *cassone* with formal geometric
inlay of ivory and fruitwood, referred to
as *certosina*. Italian, sixteenth century.
Cooper-Hewitt Museum

17

17.
Walnut *cassone* in Roman sarcophagus shape. The carving depicts a Roman triumphal procession and a shield or coat of arms. Italian, probably carved in Rome, mid-sixteenth century. Frick Collection, New York

18.
Design for a *cassone* with lion-paw feet by an unidentified artist. Caryatid figures embellish the corners. Italian, c. 1600. Cooper-Hewitt Museum

19.
Six sketches for children's beds by an unidentified artist. Robust carving dominates the Renaissance designs. Italian, c. 1630. Cooper-Hewitt Museum

20.
Table with carved marble supports and inlaid marble top. It was made for the Palazzo Farnese in Rome and possibly was designed by the architect Giacomo da Vignola. Italian, c. 1570. Metropolitan Museum of Art, New York, Dick Fund, 1958

18

21

22

for ceremonial functions. Two types of cradles were popular during the Renaissance: one had rockers that were set into rectangular cuts in the bottoms of the legs (plate 19); the other consisted of a basket-like device that was suspended between two lateral posts.

The *credenza* also reached new heights of design during the Italian Renaissance. This variation of a side table first appeared during the Gothic period and probably had its origins in the furniture supplied to medieval religious orders. Eventually, it became a sideboard for the display of opulent gold and silver vessels and dishes. The lower section could be closed with a pair of doors and was occasionally equipped with one or more drawers. In northern Europe it developed into a buffet-sideboard called a *stollenschrank*. In both Italy and northern Europe such pieces were later replaced by a cupboardlike affair with additional open shelves at the top that provided a showcase for prized possessions.

In a departure from medieval custom, tables no longer were taken down immediately after use but were a permanent part of the furnishings. Since they had become an integral part of the interior architecture of grand rooms, tables now were elaborately carved or embellished with other forms of rich decoration. Frequently tabletops were made from slabs of veined and colored marble, often inlaid with semiprecious stones of contrasting colors. These tops were mounted on mammoth carved stone supports (plate 20), making it impossible to move the table easily.

Chairs, too, changed during the Renaissance. Folding chairs began to lose favor as permanent residences became more commonplace. However, an inventory of the possessions of Catherine de Médicis taken in 1589 reveals that she owned several X-shaped folding chairs with reclining backs, of the sort generally reserved for the most important person in the household, similar to the stationary example in plate 21. Lavish carved embellishment transformed simple wooden chairs into works of art (plates 22 and 23). Rich inlay, dazzling mosaics and mother-of-pearl decorative motifs were profusely applied. During the late Renaissance, chairs constructed from turned members achieved great popularity.

Italian Renaissance decoration is characterized by its use of classical ornament, frequently based upon the five Roman architectural orders but also including a classical vocabulary of carved masks, trophies, grotesques and acanthus leaves derived from Roman examples. Although the centers of furniture design were adopting Renaissance ideals as the latest fashion, Gothic traditions lasted longer in isolated rural areas.

In northern Europe the Renaissance was not accepted with equal speed in all countries. For example, German acceptance of Renaissance precepts came slowly, and Gothic prototypes prevailed in Germany over several centuries. German furniture makers began to ac-

21.
Walnut Savonarola chair, named after the martyr Girolamo Savonarola. The names of famous Renaissance Italians are used today to describe several different types of chairs. Italian, sixteenth century. Cooper-Hewitt Museum, gift of Harvey Smith

22.
Walnut *sgabello* chair. The seat on chairs of this type was sometimes hinged so that it could be lifted up to permit access to a small storage space. The boxlike section under the seat was mounted on solid front and back supports instead of legs. Italian, sixteenth century. Cooper-Hewitt Museum, gift of Charles W. Gould

23.
Four sketches for high-backed Renaissance-style armchairs by an unidentified seventeenth-century artist. Variations of ornament are shown in the designs. Italian, 1600–1650. Cooper-Hewitt Museum

23

knowledge the new style sometime during the third quarter of the sixteenth century, and from that time on they relied heavily upon classical designs for their inspiration.

Probably the most significant Renaissance invention was the printing press. By the end of the fifteenth century, use of the press had spread throughout western Europe, and during the first half of the sixteenth century furniture designs were published at Zurich, Antwerp and Nuremberg. Among the northern designers whose Renaissance designs were transmitted throughout Germany, Peter Flötner (1490/95–1546), of Nuremberg, is one of the most famous. His wardrobe designs were used frequently by anonymous furniture carvers and joiners. Wardrobes with three-dimensional sculptural embellishments became popular in Germany soon after the opening of the sixteenth century. The general trend toward exuberant decoration increased.

Augsburg, since the development of its sawmill in 1322, had been a significant cabinetmaking center. During the Renaissance cabinets and cupboards were created there in vast numbers both for the domestic market and for export. These dazzling showpieces displayed a wealth of ornament and were much sought after by rulers, including Charles V, who ordered an extraordinary writing table from Lienhart Strohmeier in 1554. The Augsburg pieces displayed technical capabilities seldom before achieved in furniture design, but they were created more for the eye than for daily use. In general, though German furniture was lavish, it failed to provide real comfort.

A lack of unified design might well be considered one of the weakest points of German Renaissance furniture. Combinations of embellishments—which often included both Gothic and Renaissance motifs on

24.
Oak buffet-cabinet decorated with carved Gothic detail. Made in two parts, it incorporates drawers below the cabinet doors. Northern Netherlands, sixteenth century. Rijksmuseum, Amsterdam

a single piece—were used from the late Renaissance to the opening of the seventeenth century.

Forms proliferated and cupboards, cabinets and other storage units were nearly as diverse as the numbers of cabinetmakers working at any given time. Their form and style varied from geographic region to region. Oak continued to be the favorite wood for northern German furniture throughout the Renaissance and well into the eighteenth century. Southern German cabinetmakers often used softwoods as well.

During the Renaissance the Low Countries (or the Netherlands) experienced disruptive wars that led in the north to the formation of a Protestant union of seven provinces in 1579. This northern area, still referred to as the Netherlands (also called Holland), became independent from the Catholic provinces in the south, which continued under Habsburg rule and came to be called Belgium.

Inhabitants of the northern provinces favored simpler furniture forms than those that were popular in the southern provinces, which acknowledged ornate Italian decorative motifs. In the port city of Antwerp, one of the most significant international commercial and cultural cities in Europe, *strapwork* decoration was used by skillful cabinetmakers to produce a three-dimensional form of decoration resulting in a lacelike surface.

Netherlandish furniture designs received great attention through their publication, and Hans Vredeman de Vries (1527–1617) and Crispyn de Passe (1564–1637) were among the most important designers for the furniture craftsmen working during this period.

The most characteristic furniture form was a two-tiered architectural buffet-cabinet embellished with richly carved ornamental motifs (plate 24), among which the lion head holding a ring was especially popular. A document from 1462 indicates that there were eleven different types of buffets in use at the time. Turnings became more ornate, and turned chairs in a myriad of forms began to appear.

By the fifteenth century Netherlandish chests were being crafted in sufficient numbers for them to be exported to a wide European market. In 1483 the English guild of coffer makers considered these imported pieces such a threat to the livelihood of its members that it succeeded in obtaining an act of Parliament forbidding their importation. Though the law was passed, it was never truly effective.

Because the Netherlanders were especially fond of paintings, secondary sources of information about furniture and furniture design abound. Renaissance paintings of the period very frequently included mammoth two-door wardrobes, or *kases*, which continued in popularity over a long period of time and were transported by the Netherlanders to their colonies wherever they were established.

During the sixteenth century France emerged as a significant center of taste, and French craftsmen began to influence furniture design in much of the Western world. Renaissance ornaments in the form of carved naturalistic vinelike motifs and classical heads became popular (plate 25). Because of the Gallic appreciation for it, the female figure was included in furniture decoration (plate 26).

French furniture assumed its own character during the reign of Henry II (1547–59), when the concepts of mannerism (a style incorporating spatial incongruities and excessively elongated human forms), introduced into France by Italian painters working at Fontainebleau, evolved into a new, specifically French school. The decoration on French furniture of the period can be described as more sinuous and fluid than its Italian counterpart. The designer Jacques-Androuet Du Cerceau (c. 1515–1585) was instrumental in this movement, and his highly individual, inventive designs often served as a source of inspiration for furniture ornamentation (plate 27 and colorplate 6). The Du Cerceau, or mannerist, style reached its highest development in Burgundy, western Switzerland and southern France.

In Dijon another master, Hugues Sambin (c. 1515–1600), also worked in a highly personal style. He embellished the cases of dressers

25

25.
Carved walnut cupboard inset with panels of marble. The base rests on bulbous turned feet. The carved decorative masks are typical of French Renaissance furniture decoration. French, c. 1570. Victoria and Albert Museum, London

26.
Carved walnut cupboard made in two sections. The human and half-human figures provide a highly sculptural feeling. The piece was made in Jujurieux, near Lyons, in France, and the original lining has the date 1591 on it. Rijksmuseum, Amsterdam

27.
Elaborately carved walnut cupboard showing the influence of both Jacques-Androuet Du Cerceau and Hugues Sambin. Carvings of fantastic creatures, bosses and strapwork are all used in the overblown detail. French, 1575–1600. Frick Collection, New York

26

27

28

28.
Carved walnut armchair inlaid with panels of ebony. This chair is easy to move because of its lightness. Sometimes chairs of similar design have padded seats and backrests covered in luxurious fabrics. French, c. 1590. Frick Collection, New York

29.
Court cupboard made of oak and walnut inlaid with sycamore and holly. "Cup and cover" carved baluster turnings are clearly visible. The piece has a closed area on the second tier. English, late sixteenth century. Metropolitan Museum of Art, New York, gift of Irwin Untermyer, 1964

and writing cabinets with consciously contrived grotesque ornamentation. Sambin's designs were published in 1572, and on the basis of similarity between actual pieces and his sketches, many examples have been attributed to his flourishing workshop.

The French love of luxury soon brought about the introduction of small occasional tables that could be conveniently used. French chairs of the late Renaissance differed from their Italian counterparts in that they were lighter, more delicately carved and more richly embellished (plate 28).

Not surprisingly, since the sixteenth century marked a high point in Spanish history, Spanish cabinetmakers were then at their most inventive. Numerous forms were developed that served as prototypes for much of the seventeenth and eighteenth centuries. These included a leather-covered armchair, or *sillón de fraileros*; a large writing box, or *papeleira* (plate 38, see page 60); and a more massive form of writing box that sat on a table with legs. The most popular writing box, however, was the *vargueño* (colorplate 11, see page 61), a desklike affair that rested on a cupboardlike base, or *taquillón*, or on a trestle stand. This ingenious device had a fall front and contained numerous compartments and drawers of varying sizes. The box itself was usually coarsely assembled and made elegant by a gilded or polychrome-covered surface.

In England importation of Renaissance designs, particularly for the carved decoration of furniture and woodwork, occurred during the reign of Henry VIII (1509–47). However, medieval forms persisted, and it is not unusual to find English sixteenth-century furniture that combines both Gothic motifs and classical devices based upon Italian prototypes.

The sturdy functional forms of chests, chairs, stools and tables remained popular in England throughout the century, each form gradually undergoing decorative changes that reflected English awareness of the newly fashionable classical style. Certain forms of furniture grew in importance, such as the three-tiered court cupboard (plate 29) that sometimes had three open shelves for the display of silver or gilt vessels. As in Italy, the bed assumed new proportions and grandeur in the houses of the wealthy, and it was often fully covered by a coffered wood canopy supported on four massive bulbous turned posts.

During this period, and also during the reign of Elizabeth I (1558–1603), England remained in close contact with the cities in the Low Countries and Germany that were centers of northern Renaissance design. English patterns for furniture and decoration can often be related to the books of designs published in those active cities.

Regardless of political and artistic isolation, by the end of the sixteenth century Renaissance concepts extended to nearly all European countries and their colonial settlements in the New World.

For the ambitious collector, Renaissance furniture can still be acquired. Though it rarely reaches the marketplace and commands high prices when it does, it was originally created in sufficient quantity for many fine pieces to have survived.

29

5   The Baroque

During the early seventeenth century the baroque style, characterized by exuberant ornamentation, emerged in Europe when the highly mannered classical designs of the late Italian Renaissance were set aside. There was a noticeable increase in the production of all the decorative arts, especially furniture, which was consciously made more comfortable through the increased use of fabric and upholstery. Newly centralized monarchies encouraged economic stability by establishing favorable trade regulations. This led to the rise of an ever-expanding middle class, which sought furniture with a much broader range of artistic and technical quality than before.

By the mid-seventeenth century flamboyant carved, painted and gilded furniture, lavishly encrusted with cupids and *putti* and bulging with acanthus leaves, shells, fruit and energetic scrolls, heralded a new fashion. Makers of baroque furniture were masters at uniting unrelated surface areas into a harmonious overall effect (colorplate 8 and plates 30 and 31).

The French Louis XIV style is thought to have been influenced by Roman baroque clerical art, which was transmitted to France by French artists and architects returning home after studying in Rome. During the time that France emerged as the world's tastemaker, several social changes occurred. Rulers with absolute power, such as the Sun King, Louis XIV (reigned 1643–1715), built gigantic palaces and castles that became the core of court and national social and political life. Specialization of rooms increased, and new furniture forms developed that had a specific use in a specific room. King Louis XIV, his economic adviser Jean-Baptiste Colbert and the painter Charles Le Brun promulgated and refined France's version of baroque design and exerted far-reaching influence on all the decorative arts. Louis's demand for lavish furniture and fine craftsmanship spurred a new magnificence in furniture design.

Colorplate 8.
Showcase on stand used to display ceramics and other treasured objects. It is made of carved and gilded walnut and limewood. Typical of baroque design are the nude gilded figures and the scrolls. Italian, late seventeenth century. Metropolitan Museum of Art, New York, gift of Madame Lilliana Teruzzi, 1972

30

30.
Armchair of carved and gilded wood with silk damask upholstery. This is an example of baroque formal furniture designed for court use. French, c. 1680. Musée des Arts Décoratifs, Paris

31.
Carved and gilded wood pedestal, or *torchère*. Pieces such as this held candlesticks or vases in a formal Louis XIV interior. French, c. 1690. Musée des Arts Décoratifs, Paris

Jean-Baptiste Colbert (1619–1683) developed national industries that supplied the French with wares previously available only through importation. He personally supervised every aspect of craft and industry in the nation in order to make certain that French products were of unequaled quality. As a result of the highly organized guild structure that was thus encouraged, furniture makers, as well as workers in other trades, were required to sign their works, thereby establishing responsibility for craftsmanship.

Charles Le Brun (1619–1690) was first and foremost a painter, but his artistic activities in the related decorative arts became a major factor in France's emergence as an arbiter of taste for Europe. Colbert recommended that Le Brun be appointed director of the Manufacture Royale des Meubles de la Couronne, established in 1667. In this position Le Brun also had responsibility for the Gobelins textile manufactory, which Colbert had purchased in 1662 for Louis XIV and transformed into a general upholstery manufactory. These combined manufactures employed carpenters, cabinetmakers, upholsterers, weavers, goldsmiths, engravers and wood and stone sculptors. Directing these workers, Le Brun exerted enormous influence over the furnishings for all the palaces owned by the king. He designed sumptuous furniture, executed elaborate decorative panels, prepared complex designs for stucco cornices for monumental ceilings and created cartoons, or sketches, for ornamental tapestries.

Le Brun's plans for the decoration and furnishing of interiors in the Louis XIV, or French baroque, style covered all the necessities of court life, from carpets and tapestries to ceramics and silver. The king had a penchant for extravagant, finely wrought, ornate metals, and Le Brun designed for Versailles numerous full-scale pieces of furniture, including tables, chairs, benches and seats, made from solid silver. A newspaper of the time, *Le Mercure Galant*, observed: "What was made of wood anywhere else would, at Versailles, be made of silver." Even Louis's eight-foot-high throne was completely wrought in ornate silver, providing an appropriate dais upon which the Sun King could shine.

New technical advances in the manufacture of glass led to the establishment of the Manufacture Royale des Glaces à Miroir in 1665, where sheets of glass of unprecedented size were created. This glass enabled French cabinetmakers to fashion monumental mirrors that had previously been technically unachievable. These large pieces reflected the splendor of court interiors.

The baroque court style reached its zenith in the work of Domenico Cucci (d. 1705) and André-Charles Boulle (1642–1732). Cucci emigrated from Italy to Paris in 1660 and worked as a cabinetmaker and goldsmith for Cardinal Mazarin, who had a taste for furniture inlaid with marble, precious stones and rare woods. Cucci further embellished much of his furniture with mounts and friezes in gilt bronze, which not only protected the corners but provided more ornamentation.

Boulle, an innovator of unequaled talents, was one of the Sun King's most important craftsmen. This artisan was discovered by Colbert, who suggested that Louis XIV establish him in his own studio at the Louvre, where he could work exclusively for the king.

Boulle's cabinet pieces are characterized by handsome panels inlaid with tortoiseshell and metal arabesques, figures and complex floral motifs. Boulle also used ivory, mother-of-pearl and exotic woods to complete many of his intricate designs. His furniture was enriched even further by elaborate and finely chased gilt-bronze mounts of many forms, for example, winged female figures. Boulle either created these mounts himself or ordered them from bronze founders. Through

Colorplate 9.
Commode with marquetry of brass and
tortoiseshell and gilt-bronze mounts; one
of a pair made by André-Charles Boulle
for the bedchamber of Louis XIV in the
Grand Trianon at Versailles. French,
1708/9. Château de Versailles

the efforts of numerous fine cabinetmakers working in France, and with the aid of Boulle's inspiration, the chest of drawers, or *commode*, developed from a small cofferlike chest into a fully realized sculptural chest of drawers (colorplate 9). This new furniture form all but replaced the earlier form of the wardrobe, which now survived primarily in rural areas. Boulle retired in 1715, and his four sons continued the workshop.

Boulle's techniques were borrowed by other craftsmen, including the much older Jean Macé, who had worked and lived in the Louvre for eight years, beginning in 1664. Acclaimed for his skillful use of floral marquetry, Macé is noted also for his furniture with superlative ebony veneer (plate 32).

Lacquered furniture imported from the Far East inspired countless reproductions by French craftsmen. Visions of the mythical Cathay, as China was called, the charming and romanticized land of poets, historians and porcelain painters, were first introduced through tales told by such visitors to Asia as Marco Polo, a Venetian who traveled there between 1271 and 1295. By the mid-seventeenth century these stories had inspired an absolute craze for Oriental designs, or at least for the European imitations of them that came to be called *chinoiserie*.

Appreciation for authentic Oriental designs and European chinoiserie greatly increased with Louis XIV's erection of a pavilion, the Trianon de porcelaine, for his favorite, Madame de Montespan. Designed by Louis Le Vau, court architect, the pavilion was begun in the park at Versailles in 1670. Though it stood for only seventeen years and was demolished in 1687, it inspired similar structures throughout all Europe during the following century.

Louis's taste for Oriental objects had, at least in part, an economic basis. When he was forced to melt down much of his ornate pure silver furniture to finance the country's long and costly wars, he found Oriental lacquer to be a welcome and relatively inexpensive substitute.

Although France replaced Italy as the most influential center of artistic creativity during the last half of the seventeenth century, this French preeminence did not totally annihilate independent developments in Italy, and a very distinct, easily recognizable, florid baroque style prevailed there for nearly two centuries.

Italian baroque furniture displayed a robust naturalistic decoration, in which plant forms were used as carved ornament (plate 33). Floral inlay was also popular, and craftsmen developed a style that remains much in vogue today. Many finely wrought cabinets were mounted on specially constructed stands that incorporated ropelike, or twisted column, legs, flat *stretchers* and *ball* or *bun feet* (plate 34). Legs of similar design were used on tables, chairs and other case pieces as well. Italian designers seemed particularly inclined to include the human figure as sculptural decoration on furniture (see plate 33 and colorplate 8).

32.
Veneered ebony cabinet. The carved relief panels show scenes from the life of the Virgin. The piece is attributed to Jean Macé of Blois. Notable baroque features include the balustrade and the spiral-turned serpentine legs. French, 1600–1650. Musée des Arts Décoratifs, Paris

33.
Armchair by Andrea Brustolon. This Venetian piece, which is made of ebony and boxwood, is part of a suite upholstered in needlework. Italian, c. 1684. Ca' Rezzonico, Venice

34.
Ebony cabinet-on-stand inlaid with *pietre dure* (ornamental work in such hardstone as agate or jasper). The cabinet, with broken pediment and balustrade, rests on a separate stand with spiral-twist legs. The inlaid decoration depicts birds and flowers. Italian, seventeenth century. Palazzo Vecchio/Palazzo della Signoria, Florence

35.
Architectural cabinet-on-stand made of
ebony, ivory, alabaster and bronze. It
comes from the Medici collections and
was executed in the Grand Ducal workshops in Florence under the supervision
of G. B. Foggini. Italian, early eighteenth
century. Palazzo Pitti, Florence

The Italian Renaissance practice of having well-known artists decorate fine furniture continued into the baroque period, and examples with landscape scenes (colorplate 10) are occasionally available to collectors today.

During the early eighteenth century painted pieces were eclipsed by complex architectural forms that showed a renewed interest in classicism. A cabinet (plate 35) that incorporates alabaster columns with Ionic capitals and seminude classical figures is a prime example.

Baroque furniture began to appear in the Low Countries in the 1620s, and here it was only slightly different in design from late Renaissance pieces. Oak cupboards with four doors and X-shaped chairs with velvet or leather seats and backs were now embellished with naturalistic and lively decorative motifs.

Dutch furniture was often simpler than its French and Italian counterparts, and molded panels were preferred as a decorative scheme by potential customers such as the burghers, who viewed vigorously carved ornament as excessive. *Broken pediments* (whose lines are broken before reaching the apex) framed by ornate heavy moldings topped many different kinds of architectural pieces, including cupboards and cabinets.

The introduction of tea from the Orient into Europe in the early seventeenth century by the Dutch East India Company gave rise to the new custom of tea drinking—inspiring many specialized pieces of furniture to accommodate it. Small tables were designed to hold cups, saucers and pots, and tea stands were made for kettles and silver urns.

Toward the end of the seventeenth century in the Low Countries, marquetry decoration on ornately veneered walnut, ebony and tortoiseshell surfaces became commonplace (colorplate 1, see page 6). During this same period appreciation for carved furniture increased, and the *cabriole leg* (a leg that curved out at the top, then in, then out at the bottom), sometimes with a carved animal-paw foot, appeared. The burgomaster's chair in plate 36, which was made in the Dutch East Indies for export to Europe, incorporates these features but in the back also includes oval panels with a decided Oriental air. As the eighteenth century opened, ornately carved furniture again faded from popularity and was replaced by pieces that had a simple overall design enriched by the use of stunningly complex and beautiful floral inlays. The cabriole leg was simplified and made more graceful with a *pad* or a *cushioned pad foot* (plate 37).

The only countries in western Europe that seem to have been little interested in the fashion of chinoiserie during the first half of the seventeenth century were Portugal and Spain, even though both were intimately connected with the Orient through the China trade.

Colorplate 10.
Harpsichord and stool of carved, painted and gilded wood. The pastoral landscape painted on the lid is attributed to Crescenzio Onofri. Italian, late seventeenth century. Metropolitan Museum of Art, New York, gift of Madame Lilliana Teruzzi, 1971

36

37

36.
Walnut swivel chair of the burgomaster type. The back and seat swivel on the base. The cutout oval panels in the back have an Oriental feeling. Made in the Dutch East Indies for export, late seventeenth century. Cooper-Hewitt Museum, gift of Alfred G. Burnham

37.
Folding bed-chair made of mahogany with floral inlay of various woods (above, closed; opposite page, open). Both French and English influences are apparent in the design. The arrangement of the movable parts is ingenious. Over the centuries the cushioned pad feet have worn down. Dutch, c. 1700. Cooper-Hewitt Museum, gift of Mrs. Abram Stevens Hewitt

Spanish craftsmen preferred traditional forms, and most Spanish baroque furniture was simple in design, relying upon intricately wrought metalwork for much of its decorative effect. No piece is more typical than the *vargueño* (colorplate 11), which had first become popular in the sixteenth century. A second type of desk, the *papeleira*, also first popular in the sixteenth century, was a form of *vargueño* constructed without a fall front (plate 38). Another traditional form made in baroque Spain was the *stretcher-base table* (plate 39).

Throughout the seventeenth and eighteenth centuries, Spanish Colonial furniture in America mirrored the styles popular in the homeland. The side chair in plate 40, for example, is from Mexico and has carved masks on the knees of the cabriole legs. In true Spanish fashion it is upholstered with leather held in place by metal tacks and pierced rosettes.

German cabinetmakers shared the Dutch enthusiasm for cabinet pieces with marquetry. They produced countless tables, chests, cabinets and cupboards that displayed craftsmanship fully equal to that of the Dutch prototypes. Chests often contained formal achitectural details as well (colorplate 12).

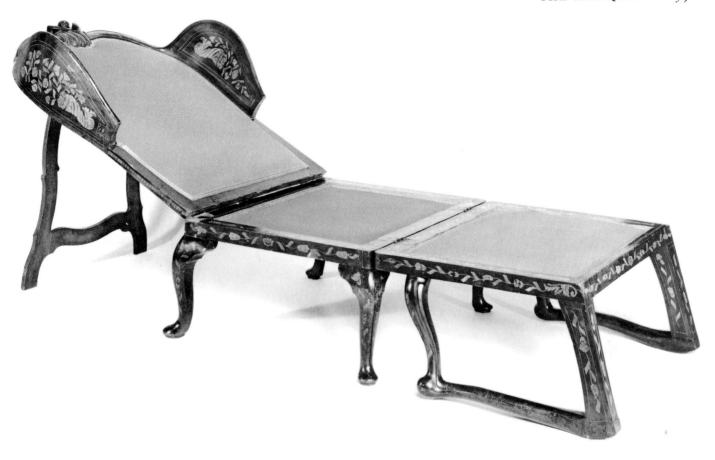

Germany's leading craftsmen enjoyed a far-reaching reputation, and monarchs in other European countries often commissioned furniture from them. A silver throne (plate 41) with an embroidered cover bearing the cipher of King Frederick IV of Denmark surmounted by the Danish royal arms, though unmarked, is believed to have been made at Augsburg in the workshop of Hieronymous Mitnacht and J. Bartermann. This splendid chair contrasts with the peasant piece in plate 42, which is from either Germany or Switzerland and which is indistinguishable from similar pieces made in America by settlers from the Rhineland.

Until 1660, when Oliver Cromwell's Commonwealth was replaced by the Stuart monarchy of Charles II (1660–85), English furniture remained medieval in form and Renaissance in decoration. Turned chairs (plate 43), so popular during the Middle Ages, continued to be produced until the end of the seventeenth century.

Charles, returning to England after a decade of exile in France, brought with him a taste for the baroque style, which was currently flourishing in France and Holland. He admired Dutch designs in particular and was convinced that the elegant and refined baroque

Colorplate 11.
Vargueño on a trestle stand. Metal mounts are placed against velvet to give a particularly rich appearance. The interior of this writing box, an early form of fall-front desk, contains many small drawers. Spanish, sixteenth–seventeenth century. Cooper-Hewitt Museum, gift of Harvey Smith

Colorplate 12.
Chest with elaborate marquetry inlay. Such chests were made in large numbers in Germany and often contained formal architectural details as decorative elements. Probably German, late sixteenth–early seventeenth century. Cooper-Hewitt Museum, gift of Mr. and Mrs. Hugh J. Grant

38.
Papeleira, a type of *vargueño* that does not have a fall front. Here the elaborately carved drawers form the chief decorative emphasis, and metal rings are provided for moving the piece. Spanish, sixteenth–seventeenth century. Cooper-Hewitt Museum, gift of Harvey Smith

38

Colorplate 11

Colorplate 12

39.
Walnut stretcher-base table. The only decorative carving appears on the three drawer fronts. Spanish, early seventeenth century. Hispanic Society of America, New York

40.
Side chair with leather upholstery. This piece illustrates the interpretation of European design elements in the New World by native craftsmen who did not completely understand the source. The carved masks on the legs are a dramatic blending of Old and New World design. Mexican, early eighteenth century. Hispanic Society of America, New York

41.
Silver throne made for King Frederick IV of Denmark by German craftsmen. This piece is a rare survival, since most silver furniture was melted down when the precious metal was needed as currency. German, c. 1715. The Royal Collection of Rosenborg Castle, Denmark

42.
Fruitwood side chair of peasant type. Chairs such as this have been made in central Europe since the late Middle Ages. They also became popular in America when the Germans settled there in the eighteenth century. German or Swiss, seventeenth century. Cooper-Hewitt Museum, gift of Harvey Smith

43.
The individual parts of this oak turned, or "thrown," chair were shaped on a lathe. In England, turners made chairs in this style from the Middle Ages until the end of the seventeenth century. English, 1600–1650. Victoria and Albert Museum, London

39

40

42

41

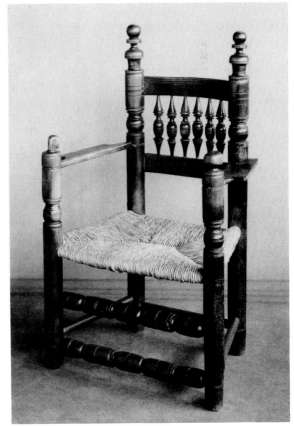

43

44.

44.
Court cupboard made of bulletwood and satinwood with inlaid panels of semi-precious stones. This traditional open style of cupboard has elaborate supports carved as female figures and heraldic animals. The feet and bottom shelf are replacements made at a later date. English, early seventeenth century. Victoria and Albert Museum, London

45.
Japanned cabinet-on-stand. The cabinet is lacquered to imitate pieces made in the Orient. The elaborate silvered stand was especially made to be used with it. English, c. 1675. Victoria and Albert Museum, London

45

furniture was more desirable than the heavier traditional forms in use throughout England (plate 44). The monumental furniture of earlier periods was quickly discarded at court and among the aristocracy and replaced by graceful, easily movable and more comfortable pieces. Numerous foreign craftsmen followed Charles to the English court, since a new and enthusiastic market for their products was also created by his homecoming. The resulting acceptance of the baroque style by English craftsmen all but eradicated the traditional designs to which they had clung so tenaciously for centuries.

46.
Writing cabinet-on-stand. The veneer is heavily burled. Contemporary inventories refer to such pieces as "scriptors." English, c. 1675. Victoria and Albert Museum, London

Authentic Chinese furniture in the form of lacquered cabinets with gilded raised designs had been imported into England and other trading countries in the early 1600s. For example, in 1613 Princess Elizabeth of England, daughter of James I, was given as a wedding present a "cabinet of China worke." The English interest in Oriental objects during the seventeenth century was so intense that when pieces were imported by the English East India Company, the directors of the organization rushed to the docks and indiscriminately grabbed any and every exotic object that could be turned to profit. Their avari-

cious actions created such a public scandal that the governor of the
company was forced to require in 1613 "that measures be taken to stop
the clamor; whereupon some of the committees promised to return
to the warehouse what they had. Twenty pieces of calico were placed
at the disposal of the Governor for presentation to the Lord Admiral
and other applicants." When the *Clove*, the first English ship to sail
to Japan, returned in 1618, more stringent policies were in effect and
the "Japanese wares, scritoires, Trunkes, Beoubes [screens], Cupps,
and dishes of all sorts, and of the most excellent varnished" were
unloaded in good order. The lacquered furniture was purposely held
back and sold slowly, thus bringing exceedingly high prices.

By 1650 English interest in the Far East was widespread. Silver or
gilt stands were fashioned locally for imported Oriental cabinets as
well as for domestic chinoiserie ones. These stands, which exemplified
baroque design, consisted of a combination of naturalistic leaves, scrolls
and plant forms with grotesque carvings of half-human, half-fantastic
figures (plate 45).

Further impetus for acceptance of the baroque style in England
came on May 21, 1662, when Charles II wed Catherine of Braganza
from Portugal. His fabulous queen brought with her not only one of
the richest dowries Europe had ever known but also a large retinue of
craftsmen including the furniture makers who introduced the *C-scroll*
and *S-scroll* motifs that were to become so popular during the last
quarter of the seventeenth century (colorplate 14). Part of Catherine's
dowry was an agreement that extended to English ships the privilege
of free trading rights in Brazil and the Portuguese East Indies. The
Portuguese possessions of Bombay and Tangiers were ceded to
England at the same time. Bombay, a west coast Indian port, gave
England a distinct advantage in establishing trade routes with both
China and the East Indies. Catherine's Indian lacquer cabinets and
other furnishings had never before been seen in England. The English
court, amazed, delighted and envious, developed a great desire to own
similar rarities.

John Stalker and George Parker in 1688 published in London
their far-reaching *Treatise of Japanning and Varnishing*, which dealt
with the creation of japanned decoration, an imitation of Oriental
lacquering. This book explained how to create fine lacquer surfaces;
it gave hints on the development of the three-dimensional pictorial
foregrounds made up of a plaster and glue mixture (today called
gesso); and it included numerous designs that the authors freely
admitted they had helped "a little in their proportions, where they
were lame or defective, and made them more pleasant yet altogether
as Antick."

Japanning was not the exclusive prerogative of professionals, for
its secrets were revealed to young ladies in finishing schools. In 1689
Edmund Verney enrolled his daughter in an "extra" course at school

Colorplate 13.
Walnut cabinet-on-stand in a transitional
style from William and Mary to Queen
Anne. The floral marquetry inlay is
especially noteworthy. English, c. 1700.
Cooper-Hewitt Museum, bequest of Mrs.
John Innes Kane

Colorplate 14.
Walnut William and Mary stool. The
slip seat is upholstered with tapestry.
The exaggerated curves in the legs and
stretchers in the form of carved C-scrolls
are typical of William and Mary style.
English, c. 1690. Cooper-Hewitt Museum,
bequest of Mrs. John Innes Kane

COLORPLATE 13

COLORPLATE 14

47.
Armchair, or easy chair, with walnut cabriole legs and colorful period needlework. The chair is a typical example of this William and Mary form, although it dates from a later period. English, c. 1715. Victoria and Albert Museum, London

48.
Pair of walnut side chairs with cane panels and velvet upholstery. The trumpet-shaped turnings of the legs identify them as late seventeenth century. The shell motifs on the pierced stretchers are common decorative devices on baroque furniture. English, c. 1690. Cooper-Hewitt Museum, gift of Irwin Untermyer

49.
Carved walnut daybed. The back resembles a chair back, and cane is used in the seat for added comfort. A pad for the seat and a cushion for the back would have been used. English, c. 1690. Victoria and Albert Museum, London

48

47

and wrote to her: "I find you have a desire to learn Jappan, as you call it, and I approve it; and so I shall of anything that is good and virtuous, therefore learn in God's name all Good Things, and I will willingly be at the charge so Farr as I am able—though they come from Japan and from never so farr and looks of an Indian Hue and colour, for I admire all accomplishments that will render you considerable and Lovely in the sight of God and man."

At the English court and in the major centers of cabinetmaking, a taste for walnut and walnut veneer emerged during the last half of the seventeenth century. Chests, cupboards, desks with fall fronts and other case pieces were made more colorful through the use of inlay, veneering (plate 46) and marquetry (colorplate 13). Especially popular were veneers of burl walnut, a decorative, highly figured wood derived from an excrescence on the trunk or branch of a walnut tree.

Parquetry, already developed to a high degree by Boulle in France and by countless Dutch cabinetmakers in Holland, was also used, but never reached the same degree of acceptance.

In 1689 James II, King of England, was exiled to France. The Dutchman William III, Prince of Orange, and his wife, Princess Mary, daughter of James II and heiress presumptive to the English throne, crossed the North Sea and ascended the throne of England. New furniture forms evolved during the reign of William and Mary (1689–94; William until 1702) and were used over an extended period of time. The easy chair (plate 47), today known as a wing chair, provided unprecedented comfort because of its upholstery and its deep wings, which served as a protection against drafts. Tall chairs that were fitted with caned backs (plate 48) and often caned seats as well were made *en suite* with a daybed, or couch (plate 49), with an adjustable back. Cane, derived from rattan, a climbing palm, was originally imported from the Orient or India. Before the end of the century English upholsterers began to protest the extensive use of cane because this flourishing branch of the furniture industry intruded upon their livelihood.

Case pieces, such as the chest of drawers with brackets or ball feet, the chest-on-frame, or highboy, and the dressing table, or lowboy, with either *S-shaped*, *cup-turned* or *trumpet-turned* legs terminating

49

50.
Interior from a house in Henrietta Place, London, designed by James Gibbs and built about 1720. The walnut Queen Anne furniture dates from the 1720s and 1730s. Victoria and Albert Museum, London

51.
Walnut reading chair upholstered in leather, with cabriole legs ending in cushioned pad feet. This form is often called a cockfighting chair, as the user could straddle the seat, push down the shelf and lean on the back while watching cockfights. But the presence of a shelf on which to rest a book and of the candle arms clearly shows that the piece was intended to be used for reading. English, c. 1720. Cooper-Hewitt Museum, gift of Mrs. Paul Moore

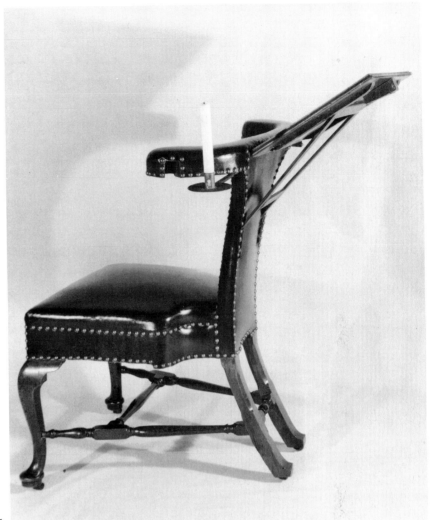

51

in ball feet, satisfied the English love for decorative embellishment because they could be finished in natural woods, veneered with exotic surfaces or further enhanced with inlay or even chinoiserie designs. Other new forms were developed because of increased literacy: the fall-front desk, the writing bureau and bookcases became important in the homes of the educated.

During the late seventeenth and early eighteenth centuries, new design elements were introduced into the furniture maker's craft. Several of them were devised by the French Huguenot Daniel Marot (1663–1752), a refugee who had sought religious freedom in Holland in 1684. He almost immediately entered the service of the Prince of Orange and followed him to England when he became

COLORPLATE 15

COLORPLATE 16

king. In 1712 Marot published a volume of engravings that exerted broad influence in Holland, England and Germany. This book included designs for chairs with cabriole legs, curvilinear backs and center splats that were oftentimes pierced and carved. Marot's engraved designs were executed by many craftsmen and inspired the general acceptance of a style that matured during the reign of Queen Anne, the second daughter of James II, who succeeded to the English throne upon the death of William III in 1702.

In terms of furniture design Queen Anne's reign (1702–14) was significant, for during this period the "foreign excesses" of the preceding decades were domesticated and totally nationalized into the cohesive English style known as Queen Anne, a style that retained its popularity for years and gave the queen's name to furniture made long after her reign (plate 50; colorplates 15, 16). Collectors should be aware that other styles also outlived their namesakes. A chair in the William and Mary style, for instance, was not necessarily made at the time the two sovereigns jointly ruled England. When attempting to date a piece, therefore, one must be sure to look for the latest characteristic discernible and not be unduly influenced by the characteristics of an earlier style.

Several design motifs borrowed from the Orient contributed to the Queen Anne style. The outline of the solid splats in the backs of chairs can be compared with the profiles of Oriental porcelain vases imported by the English East India Company. The *claw-and-ball foot* (in the form of a claw clutching a ball) is reputed to have been copied from Chinese ivory carvings of a dragon clutching a pearl.

Comfort became a keynote. The daybed, first introduced in the William and Mary period, continued in fashion. Upholstered furniture increased, and the high-backed *settee* came into general use.

Not nearly so popular as the cabriole leg with claw-and-ball foot was the cabriole leg with pad or cushioned pad foot (plate 51), a motif that did, however, enjoy favor in the English colonies in America, where it dominated furniture design from 1720 to 1755.

Under George I (reigned 1714–27) case furniture became more architectural, for it expressed the taste of contemporary architects such as William Kent (1684–1748), whose interpretations of the Italian baroque were highly individual. Kent was one of the first English architects to plan a house in a unified scheme, taking into consideration not only the architecture but the interior decoration and the furniture as well. His heavily carved and gilded furniture was decorated with shells, cornucopias, garlands of fruit and flowers, and masks—bold, exaggerated motifs that dramatically suited the heavy magnificence of his interiors. Kent's designs were translated by numerous London cabinetmakers into their own versions of the baroque style (colorplates 16 and 17).

Colorplate 15.
Walnut side chair in the taste that became popular during the reign of Queen Anne. It was made for Nicholas, the fourth and last Earl of Scarsdale, who began rebuilding and refurnishing the family house, Sutton Scarsdale, in 1724. The chair, which is part of a suite of furniture, is thought to have been made between 1724 and 1736, the date of the earl's death. On the splat is a panel of *verre églomisé* with the Scarsdale coat of arms. Cooper-Hewitt Museum, bequest of Mrs. John Innes Kane

Colorplate 16.
Queen Anne–style carved and gilded walnut side chair. The carved surface details such as the embellishments on the knees of the front legs were derived from the designs of the English architect William Kent. English, c. 1725. Metropolitan Museum of Art, New York, bequest of Irwin Untermyer, 1974

Colorplate 17.
Bureau-cabinet of walnut and burl walnut veneer inlaid with other woods showing the influence of William Kent. A strong architectural quality characterized English cabinet furniture until the third quarter of the eighteenth century. English, c. 1740. Metropolitan Museum of Art, New York, gift of Irwin Untermyer, 1964

52.
Oak trestle table with pine top. The top of this twelve-foot-long table lifts off so that the piece can be moved more easily. Trestle tables were listed in early American inventories as "table bords." American, New England, c. 1650. Metropolitan Museum of Art, New York, gift of Mrs. Russell Sage, 1909

In America indigenous furniture styles with regional variations in design evolved soon after permanent colonization. Colonists from the same country in the Old World, bound together by religious faith, tended to settle in a cultural pocket in the New World. The English dominated New England and the south; the Dutch were preeminent in the early days of New York; the Germans, the Swiss and the Swedes were among the first settlers in Pennsylvania, New Jersey and Delaware. However, in spite of ethnic differences, traditional English forms and styles permeated much of seventeenth-century American furniture design (plate 52).

In early New England, furnishings were few, for the settlers were at first concerned primarily with survival. However, it was also true that a man's wealth and social position could be measured by the quantity and quality of the furniture, pewter and silver he possessed. William Wood, writing from the Massachusetts Bay Colony in 1634, just fourteen years after the founding of the settlement, expressed a need for "an ingenious Carpenter, a cunning Joyner, a handie Cooper, such a one as can make strong ware for the use of the countrie." Edward Johnson, a professional joiner or cabinetmaker, observed in 1642: "The Lord hath been pleased to turn all the wigwams, huts, and hovels the English dwelt in at their first coming, into orderly, fair and well-built houses, well furnished many of them."

During the first fifty years of colonial settlement, American furniture followed English precedents, and consequently, as in England, most pieces were made of oak. By the 1680s other native woods better suited to serve the particular need of the furniture maker had been introduced. Decoration was of the three basic types: carved, painted and applied (plate 53). However modest and practical, American furniture of the 1620–1720 period was by no means crude, for as soon as a style became popular in Europe, a simplified interpretation of it was introduced

53.
Press cupboard of oak and pine attributed to Thomas Dennis of Ipswich, Massachusetts, one of the earliest American craftsmen of whom there is a record. Press cupboards were fitted with either shelves for linens or pegs for clothes. Their turned balusters and turned and applied spindles and bosses were usually painted black to simulate ebony. American, 1660–1700. Museum of Fine Arts, Boston, gift in memory of Mr. and Mrs. William H. Robeson

54.
William and Mary gumwood chest-on-frame, or highboy, made in New York. Gumwood was especially prevalent in the New York area. Highboys remained in general use in America long after they had disappeared in England. American, c. 1690. Metropolitan Museum of Art, New York, Rogers Fund, 1936

53

54

55

in the colonies. Furniture forms included Bible boxes, chests, chests of drawers, beds, chairs, benches, settles, cupboards and tables.

Following the restoration of the Stuart monarchy in England in 1660, furniture that incorporated twisted ropelike carved stretchers, legs and supports, typical of the baroque, came into popular favor at the English court. By 1670 this "twisted" style (plate 54) had reached American shores, where it flourished for the rest of the seventeenth century.

Because American homes were generally small, furniture with space-saving or dual-purpose qualities was especially popular. Many colonists lived, ate and slept within a single room. Some beds were constructed with a mechanism that enabled them to be folded and stored against the wall when not in use. Settles that converted into beds, chairs fashioned with backs that tipped to become table-tops (plate 55), tuckaway tables and gateleg tables (plate 56) were some of the more ingenious forms created by enterprising New World craftsmen.

In the south people of means lived in homes that closely approximated those left behind in England, and they looked to England for their best furniture. Lieutenant Colonel William Fitzhugh of Virginia wrote to London in 1681 requesting a "feather bed & furniture, curtains & vallens [valances]. The furniture, Curtains & Vallens, I would have new, but the bed at second hand, because I am informed new ones are very full of dust."

55.
Oak chair-table. The top of this dual-purpose piece moves on wooden dowels, thus enabling the homeowner to place it flat against the wall, providing more space in the room. Originally there was a drawer in the frame under the seat. American, probably made in the Guilford area of Connecticut, c. 1670. Smithsonian Institution, National Museum of History and Technology, Greenwood Gift

56.
William and Mary walnut gateleg table. It has four gates, or swing legs, which pull out to support the heavy leaves. American, New England, 1690–1720. Metropolitan Museum of Art, New York, gift of Mrs. Russell Sage, 1909

56

During the William and Mary period, Oriental design motifs were incorporated into American furniture decoration (colorplate 18). Chinoiserie became the rage among well-to-do colonials in major centers of cabinetmaking such as Boston and New York.

Some of the new forms that appeared in the last quarter of the seventeenth century were the butterfly table (a drop-leaf table with wing-shaped swinging supports for the leaves), the lowboy, the easy chair, the fall-front desk, the highboy, the mixing table, the splay-legged table and the tall cane-backed chair. The C-scroll and S-scroll, which were in general use in England at the time, became important decorative motifs in the colonies; they were used in the crest rails and matching stretchers of seating pieces.

By 1720, when the American Queen Anne period evolved, major schools of cabinetmaking had developed in several cities. Without the conservative guild system of training apprentices in traditional techniques, furniture makers developed distinctive characteristics that varied greatly from region to region; often the origin of an American piece can be determined by the method of construction, the design and the woods used. Common to all regions was the use of the cabriole leg with pad foot, which was as popular in America as the cabriole leg with claw-and-ball foot was in England at the same time. During the Queen Anne period imported mahogany began to replace native woods, and it was used in the construction of the most prized pieces. New forms included the card table with folding top, the side chair with vase-shaped splat and tea tables with dished tops and cabriole legs. Both the highboy (plate 57) and the lowboy continued in general use throughout the entire Queen Anne period. In England they were no longer fashionable and toward the end of the period had all but ceased to be made.

Americans also pursued comfort. Furniture design was altered to accommodate upholstery, and the easy "chaire" was a popular household appointment. Contemporary inventories and account books attest to the wide variety of fabrics that were imported especially for use by the upholsterer. The daybed, first introduced in the William and Mary period, continued in fashion.

The major schools of cabinetmaking that evolved during the Queen Anne period were in Boston and Newport in the north; New York and Philadelphia in the mid-Atlantic colonies; and Williamsburg and Charleston in the south.

Cabinetmakers in the cosmopolitan city of Boston and its environs were strongly influenced by English fashions. Inherent New England restraint, however, was evident in their furniture designs, which were chaste interpretations of early eighteenth-century heavily decorated English pieces (plate 58).

In Newport the Townsend-Goddard dynasty of furniture craftsmen was founded by the Quakers Job Townsend (1699–1765) and

Colorplate 18.
William and Mary japanned highboy made of maple and white pine. The chinoiserie on the drawer fronts resembles designs from Stalker and Parker's *Treatise of Japanning and Varnishing*, which was published in London in 1688. American, Massachusetts, c. 1700. Metropolitan Museum of Art, New York, purchase, Joseph Pulitzer Bequest, 1940

57.
Queen Anne cherry highboy. The brass pulls and keyhole surrounds are of a type that remained popular through the Chippendale period in America. The long, slender feet on this piece are referred to as slipper feet. The chest was made on Long Island's North Shore. American, c. 1740. Collection Raynham Hall, Oyster Bay, N.Y.

58.

Queen Anne linen press made by Ebenezer Hartshorne. The linen press, made for the storage of linen, is a rare form in American furniture. This piece has a block front in the lower section and inlaid mariner's compasses under the broken-arch pediment. Walnut, inlaid with satinwood, rosewood and oak. American, Charlestown, Massachusetts, c. 1735. Collections of Greenfield Village and the Henry Ford Museum, Dearborn, Mich., gift of the late Mrs. Edsel B. Ford in memory of Robert Hudson Tannahill

John Goddard (1723–1785). Much of their furniture was distinguished by simple lines. Their greatest pieces were enriched with shell carvings (plate 59) and block and serpentine fronts. (In the *block front* the center section is recessed behind—or extends in front of—the side sections. The *serpentine front* combines concave and convex curves.) Newport's strategic geographic location and deep natural harbor gave local furniture makers ready access to a worldwide market for the products they fashioned from native walnut and imported mahogany.

Despite the diverse nature of the population in New York, Dutch traditions continued to dominate the daily life of the colony, even after the Dutch colonial period ended in 1664, the year that the English, under the leadership of the Duke of York, deposed the peg-legged

59.
Mahogany dressing table, or lowboy, by Job Townsend. This Queen Anne piece has four pointed slipper feet, and a carved shell contained within a semicircle centers the serpentine skirt. American, Newport, Rhode Island, 1740–60. Collections of Greenfield Village and the Henry Ford Museum, Dearborn, Mich.

60

61

Peter Stuyvesant and the Dutch West India Company. Nearly ninety years later the Swedish naturalist Peter Kalm observed the lingering Dutch influence in the city of Albany: "They speak Dutch, their manners are likewise Dutch; their dress, however, is like that of the English." Mrs. Anne Grant, who wrote novels a few decades later, noted: "Valuable furniture . . . was the favorite luxury of these people." The *bodice-back chair* (plate 60) was especially popular in New York.

Philadelphia furniture of the Queen Anne period (plate 61) is more like contemporary English examples than is that from any of the other colonies. The similarities are so strong in both form and construction that even today experts disagree on the origin of many pieces.

Wealthy southern colonists, isolated by rural plantation life, were not content with furniture of domestic origin. One gentleman, writing in the early eighteenth century, noted: "From England, the Virginians take every article for convenience or ornament which they use, their own manufactures not being worth much." Despite this preference for imported goods, many excellent pieces were created by cabinetmakers in both Williamsburg and Charleston during the eighteenth century.

A Boston advertisement of 1714 attests to the popularity of Oriental taste in the colonies: "Japan Work of all sorts done and sold, at Looking Glass shop in Queen Street near the Town House." "Looking Glasses—Frames plaine, Japan'd or Flowered" were offered by Gerardus Duyckinck of New York City in 1735. Colonists appear to have relied heavily upon the Stalker and Parker English publication *Treatise of Japanning and Varnishing*, for it was included in numerous New World libraries, among them the Library Company of Philadelphia, which listed it in their 1789 catalogue.

While baroque furniture design in the New World related directly to that in England and Holland, developments in France under Philippe, Duke of Orleans, the regent who ruled immediately after the death of Louis XIV, added another dimension to the story of baroque design. One catalyst in the story was Juste-Aurèle Meissonnier (1693–1750), who popularized through his published designs the asymmetrical, organic and naturally inspired motifs that were used by furniture makers, metalsmiths and other craftsmen as well. The furniture decoration of the Louis XIV style was refined by Meissonnier and used during the Régence, as this period is known, to create exquisite sinuous forms.

Régence design reached its fullest expression at the hands of the metalworkers. Goldsmiths and bronzesmiths provided gilt mounts composed of delicately asymmetrical scrolls, shell designs and floral motifs. The furniture style that began to emerge during the Régence lasted until the middle of the eighteenth century, when it slowly evolved into the flamboyant, audacious rococo.

60.
Pair of Queen Anne walnut modified bodice-back armchairs. They are upholstered in period linen worked in colored crewels. The looped arm, a rare feature in American furniture, occurs most often on Philadelphia pieces, but these examples were made in New York. American, 1730-50. Metropolitan Museum of Art, New York, bequest of Maria P. James, 1911

61.
Queen Anne walnut settee upholstered in velvet. It was made in Philadelphia for James Logan, William Penn's secretary. The piece has *trifid* (three-toed) feet with carved shells at the knees of the cabriole legs. (Originally there was a sixth leg in the center of the front skirt, and this has recently been restored. The piece has also been reupholstered in silk and linen.) American, Philadelphia, c. 1735. Metropolitan Museum of Art, New York, Rogers Fund, 1925

6 One Hundred Years of Great Furniture Design

The French rococo style flourished in the years following the transitional period of the Régence, in which the ponderous and impressive baroque forms were gradually modified to accommodate a much more private and intimate setting. Between 1720 and 1730 the rococo style emerged as a stunning contrast to the decorative vocabulary of the previous century; however, superb craftsmanship remained as an undercurrent of stability amid these revisions in taste.

France continued to be the arbiter of style and a center for furniture design that influenced all Europe during the eighteenth century, and furniture in the rococo style is often called Louis XV, after the monarch who ruled France (1715–74) during this high point in the history of design. The room designed by Nicolas Pineau for the Hôtel de Varengeville in Paris about 1735 (see frontispiece) is a wonderful example of this unabashed style.

Rococo is characterized by elegance, lightness and remarkably executed minute decorative details, such as interlacing shells, plant and floral motifs, C-scrolls and S-scrolls. The cabriole leg, which had first become popular during the early baroque period, was further refined and the scroll foot, or *whorl foot*, was used extensively (plate 62). *Bombé* chests with swelling curvilinear bodies and serpentine fronts adorned with sculptural metallic embellishments in ormolu, bronze, silver and even gold reached their zenith in this period (plate 63).

The increasing affluence of the bourgeoisie led to increasing numbers of sumptuous dwellings, which in turn called for vast quantities of furniture of myriad forms and purposes.

Louis XV's court was dominated by his mistress, Madame de Pompadour, a former member of the bourgeois class whose wit, intelligence and sophistication gained her not only the adulation of the king but also her own apartments at Versailles. This independent and brilliant woman was influential in Louis's political decisions and had a

Colorplate 19.
Rococo sedan chair made of carved and gilded poplar and lindenwood enriched with gilt-bronze mounts. Four side panels are painted with cupids and garlands. The interior is padded, lined with velvet and decorated with gold braid, fringe and tassels. The sedan chair was both a piece of furniture and an elegant means of transportation. Italian, c. 1760. Metropolitan Museum of Art, New York, gift of J. Pierpont Morgan, 1922

62

63

62.
Side, or console, table of gilded wood with a marble top. This skillfully made piece was intended principally for display. The scroll feet are particularly noteworthy. French, c. 1740. Cooper-Hewitt Museum, gift of Mr. and Mrs. Richard Rodgers

63.
Medal cabinet in the form of a commode with a marble top, made for Louis XV by Antoine Gaudreaux. It is veneered with kingwood and elaborately mounted with gilt bronzes made by the brothers Slodtz. French, 1730. Château de Versailles

64.
Small table, or *chiffonnière*, with painted surfaces, gilt-bronze mounts and a top made of Sèvres porcelain. The piece is signed by Roger Vandercruse, who became a master craftsman in 1755. It has one drawer, under the top, which is so exquisitely integrated into the overall design as to be nearly invisible. French, c. 1760–65. Musée Nissim de Camondo, Paris

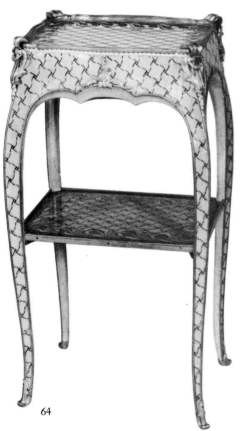

64

65

65.
Plate from Diderot's *Encyclopédie ou Dictionnaire raisonné des sciences, des arts et des métiers*, published in Paris in thirty-five volumes, 1751–80. The plate, from a volume published in 1771, shows an eighteenth-century upholsterer at work on a chair of rococo design. Cooper-Hewitt Museum Library

great effect on France's cultural life. The writer Voltaire and the painter François Boucher were among her intimate artistic friends. Boucher even served as her personal designer, portraitist and confidant for many years.

It was partially at Madame de Pompadour's urging that the king assumed ownership in 1753 of the porcelain factory at Vincennes (moved to Sèvres in 1756). Besides producing the finest and rarest soft-paste porcelain luxuries in all Europe, the Sèvres factory also contributed to French furniture making through its exquisitely painted plaques, which were often included in the decoration of furniture. Slabs of porcelain were especially crafted for tabletops (plate 64).

Both at court and in private residences, the salon, or social gathering, became a ritual. An increased concern for convenience was reflected in the development of smaller armchairs, sofas and easily movable tables that provided more flexibility. Innumerable furniture forms developed, and large suites were made up of matching tables, chairs, sofas, lounges, footstools, stools and looking glasses.

Paris continued to be the center of French cabinetmaking throughout the eighteenth century. The guild of *menuisiers-ébénistes* established strict rules governing the division of labor for members of its highly complex organization. Furniture joiners, or cabinetmakers, called *menuisiers*, were responsible for the production of everything crafted from wood, including cupboards, tables, beds and other pieces. *Menuisiers* were, however, prevented from extensive ornamental carving, which, according to guild requirements, had to be executed by members of the sculptors' guild. *Menuisiers* were allowed to use turned wood and simple carved ornament of their own design and execution. They could also attach ormolu decoration to their furniture, but they were forbidden to manufacture the ormolu objects.

Ébénistes, or master craftsmen, fashioned chairs, sofas and some of the same types of case pieces as the *menuisiers*. They frequently utilized rich veneer, sumptuous marquetry and complicated mechanisms such as drawers with fall fronts and secret compartments that could be revealed at the touch of a button. Upholsterers were also important contributors to furniture making (plate 65).

Members of the Parisian guilds were required to stamp or sign their names on pieces between the years 1743 and 1790. They also often added the mark of their corporation. These signatures and marks assist collectors today in identifying the maker of a piece. One famous master craftsman was Bernard II Vanrisamburgh, who worked from before 1730 to 1763 or 1766 (colorplate 20).

French rococo furniture was delightful in design, unequaled in craftsmanship and filled with subtle distinctions of form intended for specific purposes. A multiplicity of small tables were developed: the *bonheur-du-jour*, a tiny table topped by a miniature chest with drawers surrounding a central niche that was designed to hold ink

Colorplate 20.
Writing table made by Bernard II Vanrisamburgh, a noted French master cabinetmaker. The piece is veneered with tulipwood and inlaid with floral sprays. A gilt-bronze gallery and mounts further enrich the surface. French, 1730–66. Metropolitan Museum of Art, New York, gift of Mr. and Mrs. Charles B. Wrightsman, 1976

66

67

68

66.
The famous *bureau à cylindre* writing table known as the *bureau du Roi Louis XV*. It is veneered with marquetry of various woods and has gilded mounts, candleholders and clock. Commissioned by Louis XV, the work was begun by Jean-François Oeben and completed by his assistant, the later master craftsman Jean-Henri Riesener. The clock was made by Jean-Antoine Lépine and the bronze mounts were designed by Jean-Claude Duplessis. French, 1760–69. Château de Versailles

67.
Bergère of gilded beechwood, one of a pair made by and signed *L. Cresson*. French, c. 1765. Metropolitan Museum of Art, New York, gift of Charles Wrightsman, 1971

68.
Voyeuse chair by Jean-Baptiste Tilliard. This type of seating piece was a variation of the *bergère*, with the back, seat, arms and the rest above the crest rail upholstered. The rest enabled someone to lean over comfortably and join a conversation or watch a game of cards while standing behind a person seated in the chair. French, eighteenth century. Musée des Arts Décoratifs, Paris

and writing materials; the *chiffonnière*, a small table, sometimes having a Sèvres porcelain top, as seen in plate 64 (the term *chiffonnière* now means a narrow, high chest of drawers); the *coiffeuse*, which held wigs and hairpins; the *guéridon*, constructed to hold elegantly wrought candlesticks; the *table à la tronchin*, a form with an adjustable mechanical device that made it useful for drawing or reading while in a standing position; the *table de nuit*, a nightstand; the *poudreuse*, constructed to hold cosmetics and other beauty aids; the *servant*, a small piece designed with a metal insert in which drinks could be kept cool for intimate dining; and the *videpoche*, which was used by a man to hold his personal belongings when he went to bed.

The *secrétaire* appeared about 1730. The lower section was constructed to function as a cupboard with drawers. The top portion was fitted with a solid front that, when lowered, provided a writing surface and revealed small drawers and pigeonholes.

The desk, generally called a *bureau*, continued to be immensely popular. There were several forms, including the *bureau à cylindre* (plate 66), which had a semicircular lid that receded into the case. The *bureau en pente* featured a sloping lid. The *bureau plat* was a large writing table, frequently with drawers under the top. An alternate form of the *bureau plat* was a complex piece of furniture surmounted by tiny drawers and niches, which were crowned by a gilt clock. The *bureau en tombeau* provided working space for two people at the same time. One of the most beautiful examples of this form was made by Bernard II Vanrisamburgh for Louis XV's twin daughters.

As with tables and desks, various types of chairs were popular during the reign of Louis XV. The *meublant* was originally conceived as decorative and generally stood at the perimeter of a room. The *courant* was primarily used in the center of salons; it was relatively light and easily movable. The *bergère* (plate 67), which had first appeared during the Régence, continued to be in favor, for it was extremely comfortable. Delicately carved wooden frames, sometimes gilded but more frequently painted and gilded, were covered in handsome silk fabrics, soft-hued tapestries or meticulously worked petit point. The *bergère en commodité* was constructed so that the back was adjustable. The *bergère en confessional* had low arms that were recessed and wings attached to its back. The *tête-à-tête*, sometimes known as the *causeuse*, *confidante* or *marquise*, was a small couchlike piece for two. The *chaise longue* was an upholstered form of the early daybed and not unlike a *bergère* with an elongated seat.

The *chauffeuse*, a seating piece with a low seat mounted on short legs, had a rounded back that provided a shield against excessive heat from open fireplaces for women with bare shoulders. The *voyeuse* (plate 68) was designed especially for people who wished to look over the shoulders of a seated person, possibly to watch the

Colorplate 21.
Commode inset with Chinese lacquer panels and crowned by a pink marble top. This bombé piece is in the fully developed Louis XV, or rococo, taste. The gilt-bronze mounts add to the sense of fantasy that the piece evokes. French, c. 1755. Cooper-Hewitt Museum, bequest of George D. Widener

69.
Commode with veneered marquetry, gilt-bronze mounts and marble top. It was made by Joseph Baumhauer, a German who worked in Paris during the Louis XV period. French, 1767–72. Toledo Museum of Art, gift of Florence Scott Libbey

70.
Bombé commode with kingwood marquetry and gilt-bronze mounts. French, late eighteenth century. Victoria and Albert Museum, London

69

70

intensely competitive and popular games of cards. It enabled the spectator to lean against a stuffed cushion set on top of the back of the chair.

The rococo style reached its zenith in the elaborate commodes of the Louis XV style (plate 69 and colorplate 21). The massive forms of the Louis XIV period, created for public display and ostentation, were simplified; the ponderous ornamentation of the previous era was replaced by a lightness and delicacy dependent on meticulous workmanship and clarity of design in the midst of riotous decoration. Drawers of commodes were reduced in number, and architectural lines were softened. Decoration was in the form of polychromed marquetry and exquisite gilt-bronze mounts in the shape of naturalistic motifs, scrolls and masks. In the *commode à vantaux*, the drawers were replaced by doors that were paneled and inlaid with marquetry or lacquerwork.

During the second half of the century beds were sometimes placed lengthwise against the wall. This arrangement was made more dramatic by the use of expensive fabrics hung in draped fashion from an ornately carved crown fixed high on the wall above the bed.

Early in the eighteenth century the term *lacquer* came into general use to describe transparent and opaque varnishes. A particularly attractive translucent varnish was developed, perfected and patented by the Martin brothers, who were French artist-craftsmen, and it came to be known all over Europe as *vernis martin*. In spite of the success of this French lacquer, interest in original Chinese lacquerwork continued to be expressed by France's cabinetmakers (see colorplate 21).

The rococo began to fade in France when excavations at Herculaneum in 1738 and Pompeii in 1748 revealed much about first-century interiors and furniture and led to renewed interest in classical forms. Madame de Pompadour expressed a serious and studious interest in the more sober neoclassical style, and eventually, in part because of her influence, furniture design became increasingly restrained. The rococo pieces with their riot of decoration were slowly replaced by architectonic design, and the Louis XVI style of neoclassicism began to emerge several years before the accession of the new king in 1774.

In the Louis XVI style was contained the antithesis of the rococo. Sinuous, organic and asymmetrical design was replaced by fluting, carved friezes and other classical devices; outlines of furniture shifted away from curves toward straight lines and right angles. Marquetry continued to be popular (plate 70) and in this period reached a high degree of perfection. There was a general increase in the use of geometric parquetry designs as well.

The Louis XVI style blended with another popular style of the time called "Pompeiian" or "Etruscan," which was typified by a complex mingling of sculptural ornaments and metal and ceramic mounts (plate

Colorplate 22.
Small mahogany cupboard crafted by Étienne Avril for Marie Antoinette. Toward the end of the eighteenth century, a strong neoclassical trend was evident in the decoration of furniture. This cupboard is embellished with striking blue-and-white medallions of Sèvres porcelain. French, late eighteenth century. Château de Fontainebleau

71). Simple furniture adhering to classical proportions was executed in mahogany soon after the mid-1770s.

Marie Antoinette, Louis XVI's vivacious queen, exerted considerable influence on furniture design, for she was especially fond of small furniture that suited her *petits appartements* at her palace and at her retreat in Versailles (colorplate 22).

Furniture making in the late eighteenth century in France was dominated by many brilliant craftsmen, such as Jean-Henri Riesener (1734–1806), Jean-Guillaume Beneman (active between 1784 and 1801), Jean-Henri Martin Carlin, who became a master in 1766, and Adam Weisweiler, who became a master in 1778.

With the Revolution, France ceased to be the world arbiter of taste, and numerous cabinetmakers who had once been financially dependent upon royal circles were forced to seek new clients elsewhere. Many of them immigrated to America, where they served the rising middle class in cities such as New York, Boston and Philadelphia.

The primary centers of rococo cabinetmaking in Germany were Berlin-Potsdam, Dresden, Munich, Würzburg and the Rhineland. The craftsmen were largely influenced by the furniture of leading Parisian cabinetmakers, which had been imported into these cities. Equally important were published decorative designs that provided inspiration for craftsmen wishing to work in the latest fashion, such as those by François Cuvilliés (1695–1768), who had been sent to Paris for his early training. Cuvilliés freely interpreted the rococo style, and in his hands it achieved a new vitality.

Many of the Dresden furniture-making shops had been established during the Renaissance, and by the early eighteenth century such men as Martin Schnell (active 1710–40) were creating writing cabinets and other specialized forms of extraordinary beauty. The south German bureau-cabinet in plate 72 demonstrates the richness of German furniture during the 1730s. The complexity of its design contrasts dramatically with the more restrained marquetry of the Palatinate commode in plate 73. The Germans also appreciated lacquered furniture: tables and chairs of brilliant scarlet embellished with gold and further enriched with ormolu mounts were especially popular.

Few German cabinetmakers mastered the delicate balance between function and beauty that Abraham Roentgen (1711–1793) and his son David (1743–1807) achieved in their Neuwied workshop between 1750 and 1795 (plate 74). David, a member of the Parisian guild, skillfully combined the fashion of the day with native traditions. He strongly influenced French cabinetmaking during the latter years of the eighteenth century. His chests, bureaus and other cabinet pieces were sought by the rich and powerful throughout Europe.

During the eighteenth century Holland nurtured few cabinetmakers as well known as the French masters of the period; however, a large number of skilled craftsmen freely interpreted French fashions.

72

71.
Jewel chest by Jean-Ferdinand Schwerdfeger given to Marie Antoinette by the City of Paris. Its design is consistent with the Etruscan style and anticipates the Empire style. The caryatids representing the four seasons were probably wrought by Pierre-Philippe Thomire. The painted panels of grotesques and the plaques in blue-and-white originated in the Sèvres factory. French, late eighteenth century. Château de Versailles

72.
Bureau-cabinet with walnut veneer inlaid with ivory and rare woods. The form is baroque, but rococo decorative detail betrays a later date. South German, 1738. Victoria and Albert Museum, London

73.
Commode with marquetry panels enriched with penwork or painted decoration and bronze mounts. It presents a restrained interpretation of the rococo style. German, Palatinate region, 1730–40. Cooper-Hewitt Museum, gift of Miss Sarah Cooper Hewitt

74.
Fruitwood card and writing table made by Abraham Roentgen of Neuwied. Its function can be changed by lowering the rack and drawers into the body. German, 1750–60. Victoria and Albert Museum, London

75.
Cabinet veneered with burl walnut and inlaid with rare woods. The mirrored door panels are painted with birds in the Chinese manner. The mounts are silver, and the base is bombé. Dutch, c. 1750. Rijksmuseum, Amsterdam

73

74

75

Like the Germans, the Dutch avidly collected fine porcelains and faience. To satisfy the demand for cupboards to display these collections, local craftsmen developed a double-tiered cabinet comprised of a convex chest of drawers topped by shelves enclosed with glass doors and finished with an ornately carved cornice. There were many variations of this form (plate 75).

The baroque style perfectly suited Italian taste, and consequently cabinetmakers in Italy used the concepts of baroque design long after they had passed from favor in France. The new style was acknowledged, however, in pieces that are transitional from the baroque to the succeeding rococo (plates 76 and 77 and colorplate 23).

76.
Carved and gilded wooden throne upholstered in velvet with braid trim. The form of this Venetian piece is baroque, but some of the ornamentation is rococo. Antonio Corradini produced a design from which it probably was made. Italian, c. 1730. Ca' Rezzonico, Venice

77.
Design for a cabinet with a base shaped like a console table with drawers. The unidentified artist has included alternative suggestions, some baroque and some rococo—for example, the rope-turned pilaster on the left is baroque in style; the naturalistic carvings suggested as decorative motifs for the right pilaster are rococo. Italian, possibly Rome, 1700–1750. Cooper-Hewitt Museum

77

Colorplate 23.
Design for a bed with a canopy, drawn by an unidentified artist. The delicate sinuous carving on the canopy marks the design as transitional from baroque to rococo. Italian, 1700–1730. Cooper-Hewitt Museum

78.
Design for a side, or console, table by an unidentified artist. The four legs are composed of volutes and are connected by volute-shaped stretchers that support a cartouche. Italian, 1750–75. Cooper-Hewitt Museum

Italian furniture of the eighteenth century reflected the opulent lifestyles enjoyed by the country's leading citizens. Dazzling furnishings (colorplate 19, see page 85, and plate 78), capricious beyond description, were created for their magnificent palaces. A leading cabinetmaker was Pietro Piffetti (active 1730–79), whose extraordinary creations were both sculptural and pictorial. In Venice Andrea Brustolon (1662–1732) fashioned sumptuous pieces of exquisite delicacy.

Venice, "Queen of the Adriatic," contained an unusually large number of lacquerwork shops and was internationally known for its painted and lacquered furniture. In this colorful city the lacquer technique was perfected by the late seventeenth century, when Maximilian Misson, a visitor, noted that "the lack [lacquerwork] of Venice is usually much esteem'd and you may have some of all prices." Some of the best surviving Venetian lacquer is a complete suite of furniture con-

79.
Armchair from a large suite of green lacquered furniture. This piece is upholstered in hand-colored silk. Italian, mid-eighteenth century. Ca' Rezzonico, Venice

80.
Commode from the same suite as the armchair in plate 79. More than thirty pieces of furniture are included in this dazzling group. Italian, mid-eighteenth century. Ca' Rezzonico, Venice

sisting of consoles, chairs, looking glasses and commodes of bottle-green "japan,'" enthusiastically decorated with gilded Chinese festival scenes (plates 79 and 80).

By the mid-eighteenth century the vogue for lacquer in Venice was so great that craftsmen sought an inexpensive way of imitating it. Prints created especially for those wishing to cut out paper figures and paste them on furniture were produced in vast quantities. The cutout designs were colored, applied with glue and varnished, thus creating a pseudo-Oriental effect. Chief among the publishers of such prints was the Remondini firm at Bassano.

81.
Pair of gilded wood candlestands. Their design is attributed to William Kent, and it is thought that Benjamin Goodison made them. English, c. 1730. Elvehjem Museum of Art, purchase, Dr. C. V. Kierzkowski Fund, University of Wisconsin, Madison

82.
Pier glass of carved pine, finished with gesso and gilt. It was made for Frederick, Prince of Wales, whose rank is symbolized by the three-feathered motif that represents the ostrich-feather badge of a Prince of Wales. The piece is thought to have been designed by William Kent and made by Benjamin Goodison. English, c. 1735. Victoria and Albert Museum, London

83.
Carved wooden pier glass and console table. Paint and gilt are used to decorate the surface of both pieces. The pier glass was designed by Matthias Lock. English, c. 1745. Victoria and Albert Museum, London

84.
Carved and gilded wood looking-glass frame. In the French rococo taste, it is based on a design in plate CLXXXVIIa in the third (1762) edition of Chippendale's *Director*. English, c. 1775. Cooper-Hewitt Museum, bequest of Mrs. Mary Hayward Weir

Just as Italian cabinetmakers tenaciously clung to the baroque style, English designers and furniture makers were not quick to abandon the stately elegance of the baroque for the more whimsical rococo forms that were emanating from France. In much of William Kent's and Matthias Lock's furniture (plates 81–83) there is a decided baroque strength, exemplified by dramatically carved scrolls that are lightened by more fanciful rococo motifs, such as floral festoons and garlands.

Beginning with the reign of George II (1727–60), the French rococo became the major foreign source of inspiration for London's cabinet-makers. Batty Langley (1696–1741) and his younger brother, Thomas, architects with far-reaching reputations, published a collection of engravings in *City and Country Builder's and Workman's Treasury of Designs* in 1740. Thomas Chippendale (1718–1779), a well-established London cabinetmaker, borrowed freely from these engravings when

85.
Mahogany wardrobe with French rococo carving. The design is based on plate CIV in the second edition (1755) of Chippendale's *Director*. English, 1755–60. Cooper-Hewitt Museum, gift of Mrs. John Innes Kane

Colorplate 24.
The frame of this carved mahogany fire-screen with Fulham "Savonnerie" panel showing a parrot and a squirrel is in the French rococo style as it was interpreted in Chippendale's *Director*. Firescreens were used to deflect heat when a fire was burning in the fireplace. They were also pushed in front of the fireplace when it was not in use, to serve as a decorative element. English, c. 1755. Metropolitan Museum of Art, New York, gift of Irwin Untermyer, 1964

86

86.
The design of this mahogany organ case with its French rococo ornamentation is similar to that in plate cv in the third edition (1762) of Chippendale's *Director*. English, 1755–60. Victoria and Albert Museum, London

87.
Mahogany armchair with Chinese fretwork in its back. The scooped seat and tapering arms give a sense of comfort. English, c. 1765. Cooper-Hewitt Museum, gift of George A. Hearn

88.
Mahogany birdcage in the Gothic taste. The pointed arches and the trefoil and quatrefoil cutouts are all taken from Gothic architecture. English, second half of the eighteenth century. Cooper-Hewitt Museum, gift of Alfred G. Burnham

89.
Design for a library breakfront bookcase in the Gothic style, signed by Thomas Chippendale. The pen-and-ink and gray-wash drawing is the original from which plate xcvii in the third edition (1762) of the *Director* was taken. English, 1755–60. Cooper-Hewitt Museum, purchased in memory of the Misses Hewitt

87

88

89

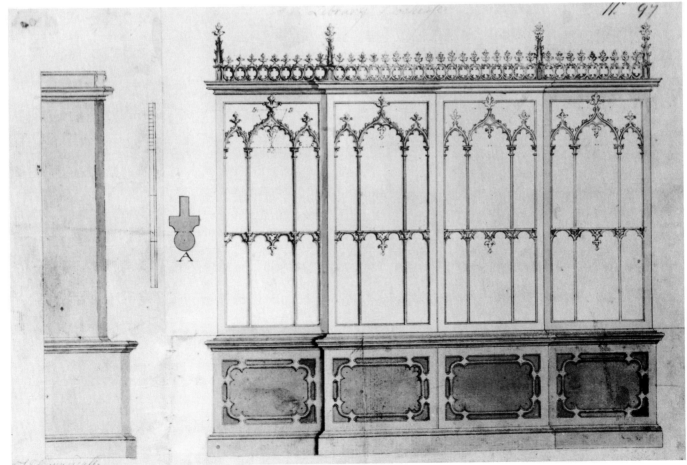

90.
Design for a medallion-back chair by
Robert Adam, dated 1779. The decorative
patterns on the back and seat were usually
painted on white satin. A similar method
of upholstery decoration was used on the
Italian chair in plate 79. English, 1779. Sir
John Soane's Museum, London

he brought out *The Gentleman and Cabinet-Maker's Director* in London in 1754, 1755 and 1762. The *Director* illustrated three primary styles: the Modern, or French rococo (plates 84–86 and colorplate 24); the Chinese (plate 87); and the Gothic (plates 88 and 89), which had been part of English tradition since the Middle Ages. Chippendale was not an innovator; he merely recorded the best furniture forms currently in vogue. His adaptations of the French rococo were probably his most important contribution. Cabinetmakers using Chippendale's sketches could create gracefully designed, elegantly restrained furniture that was, in its own way, as beautiful as the highly ornamental French rococo pieces.

Naturally, numerous other designers sought to duplicate Chippendale's successes. William Ince and John Mayhew brought out *The Universal System of Household Furniture* between 1759 and 1763, and Robert Manwaring published *The Cabinet and Chair-Maker's Real Friend and Companion* in 1765.

Robert Adam (1728–1792), Scottish architect and furniture designer, based many of his designs on classical Roman prototypes. During the 1750s Adam, like many another, moved to Italy, where he became intimately familiar with the archaeological explorations of Italian artists such as Giovanni Battista Piranesi (1720–1778). Exposure to international tastemakers provided Adam with new design ideas that he popularized in England (plate 90).

Robert Adam obtained many of the most coveted architectural commissions in England during the 1760s. He executed not only the plans for buildings but drawings for their interiors and furnishings as well.

Adam's concept of design was based upon delicacy and refinement. To assist him in his decorative work, he assembled a brilliant international group of craftsmen and artists. He discarded the baroque cabriole leg and in its place introduced a slender straight tapering leg with a *spade foot* (a foot somewhat wider than the leg, in the shape of a spade). He reintroduced the pedestal as a support for urns or candelabra. He is given credit for the development of the *sideboard*, a long cabinet with compartments and shelves for holding articles of table service, which grew out of his use of a table flanked by pedestals (colorplate 25).

Ormolu was not especially popular in England; however, Adam used it on some chairs and case pieces. He adored exotic woods and revived painted decoration and pictorial marquetry.

Adam's influence is clearly evident in two late eighteenth-century publications: George Hepplewhite's *The Cabinet-Maker and Upholsterer's Guide*, published posthumously in 1788 by his widow, Alice Hepplewhite, and *The Cabinet-Maker and Upholsterer's Drawing Book*, published in 1791–94 by Thomas Sheraton. Both these men incorporated Adam's ideas into their designs. Hepplewhite introduced

Colorplate 25.
Sideboard table and pedestals with urns designed by Robert Adam and probably executed by John Linnell. The base of the table was fashioned from softwood, which was then gilded. The top is richly figured mahogany. The accompanying pedestals and urns are painted and gilded. Adam was one of the first to combine antique shapes and create a sideboard suite for the dining room. English, 1750–75. Osterley Park, Middlesex, England

91.
Mahogany Chippendale side chair in the French rococo style. The elaborate carving on Philadelphia furniture was often done by craftsmen who had recently come from London. American, Philadelphia, 1760–70. Henry Francis du Pont Winterthur Museum, Winterthur, Del.

92.
The finest type of Philadelphia carving is in evidence on this mahogany Chippendale highboy—particularly in the vases with flowers, which serve as finials, and the panel on the base depicting a scene from *Aesop's Fables*. The piece was made in Philadelphia for the Howe family of that city. American, c. 1770. Philadelphia Museum of Art

91

92   93

shield-back chairs set on slender tapering legs, and Sheraton favored latticelike backs and slender turned and reeded legs.

During the 1790s French influence on English cabinetmakers was significant. In 1801 Charles Percier and Pierre-F.-L. Fontaine released their *Recueil de décorations intérieures*, which introduced historically inspired furniture of authentic design and proportion. English Regency designers likewise took their lead from the furniture of ancient Greece, Rome and Egypt. The *klismos* and *curule* (curved or modified X-shaped base) chairs, the tripod table and the daybed, all based on archaeological forms, could be found in many drawing rooms of even modest pretension. Greek, Roman and Egyptian motifs appeared on a multitude of furniture forms.

The American rococo was based almost exclusively upon designs from Thomas Chippendale's *The Gentleman and Cabinet-Maker's Director*. Chippendale's concepts were considered new and fashionable; soon after their introduction the Queen Anne style abruptly faded in America. In its place a simplified variation of the French rococo became popular (plate 91). The claw-and-ball foot, which had been popularized in English furniture making during the late seventeenth century, was now used by American craftsmen in the major centers of cabinetmaking at Philadelphia, Newport, Boston and New York.

Philadelphia furniture makers borrowed and freely adapted Chippendale's concepts, and through sensitive design and expert craftsmanship they created a homogeneous wealth of furniture that has come to be recognized as America's most significant contribution to world furniture. The highboy, ornamented with rich carvings of shells, vines and tendrils in both the upper and lower sections, is perhaps the supreme achievement of Philadelphia cabinetmakers. Highboys were often accompanied by matching lowboys. The highboy had been widely used in most of Europe during the early baroque period, when it was primarily a chest-on-frame, but it abated in popularity during the rococo period. This form was immensely popular in America, where numerous drawers replaced the frame, and it became a monumental case piece that was used not only in the bedroom but in the best parlors as well (plate 92).

New forms appeared during the Chippendale period. The breakfront bookcase (whose central section projects beyond the end sections), the kneehole chest of drawers (with recessed area to accommodate the knees of a sitting person), the sofa with a serpentine back, the kettle stand and the drop-leaf Pembroke table were all American adaptations of English forms.

American interpretations of the rococo were often more symmetrical than the French or the English. During the period 1755 to 1785 Job Townsend and John Goddard at Newport, the second great school of American cabinetmaking after Philadelphia, utilized a block-

93.
Mahogany Chippendale block-front secretary-bookcase from Goddard-Townsend school of cabinetmaking in Newport, Rhode Island. The block front with shells was a popular form of furniture decoration there. American, c. 1765. Yale University Art Gallery, New Haven, Conn., Mabel Brady Garvan Collection

94.
Mahogany Chippendale block-front secretary-bookcase made in Massachusetts. The block front is not as pronounced as in Newport examples. American, c. 1770. Virginia Museum of Fine Arts, Richmond, Marsh Collection

94

95

96

95.
Sheraton side table. This serving piece is fitted with a shaped marble top and decorated with gilded and painted classical motifs, including urns and two horns tied with a ribbon. American, Baltimore, 1790–1800. Collections of Greenfield Village and the Henry Ford Museum, Dearborn, Mich.

96.
Mahogany and mahogany veneer Hepplewhite card table with carving attributed to Samuel McIntire. The spade feet are painted to simulate ebony. Carvings of pendant grapes and grape leaves embellish the front legs. American, Salem, Massachusetts, 1790–1810. Collections of Greenfield Village and the Henry Ford Museum, Dearborn, Mich.

and-shell-carved design (plate 93) that rivaled the designs of the finest Philadelphia pieces. Block-and-shell-carved pieces were crafted in Connecticut and Massachusetts as well (plate 94).

Toward the end of the eighteenth century new schools of cabinet-making emerged as major cities mushroomed along the eastern sea-board. Craftsmen in Baltimore (plate 95); Salem, Massachusetts (plate 96); Portsmouth, New Hampshire; and countless other cities relied heavily upon classical designs in books published by such English cab-inetmakers and designers as Hepplewhite and Sheraton.

At the close of the eighteenth century inspiration for American furniture moved from London to Paris; consequently a new phase of classicism spread to America. The neoclassical style closely followed French Empire prototypes. New York became the center of high-style cabinetmaking, with Philadelphia and Boston close behind.

Immigrant French cabinetmakers flocked to America, the land of plenty, in their effort to avoid the devastating consequences of France's political struggles, which had brought an end to the *ancien régime*. Primary among the cabinetmakers working in the late eigh-teenth century were Charles-Honoré Lannuier (1779–1819), a French immigrant (plate 97), and Duncan Phyfe (1768–1854), a Scots immi-grant who settled first in Albany and moved later to New York City.

97.
Mahogany and rosewood veneer classical card table attributed to Charles-Honoré Lannuier. The pine monopodia, or animal-form supports, are painted and gilded. Lannuier was a French cabinet-maker who immigrated to America, where he produced exceedingly fine furniture. American, New York City, 1815–19. Collections of Greenfield Village and the Henry Ford Museum, Dearborn, Mich.

98.
Painted and decorated dower chest. The decoration on the side panels is derived from medieval illuminations and is generally associated with the Pennsylvania Germans. American, Lancaster County, Pennsylvania, c. 1780. Metropolitan Museum of Art, New York, gift of Mrs. Robert W. de Forest, 1933

99.
Windsor armchair of several different kinds of wood. Painted finishes were used to disguise the fact that craftsmen selected various woods to best suit their purpose. Usually the seats in Windsor chairs are pine, while the legs and spindles are often maple, hickory and ash. American, Massachusetts, 1780–1800. Yale University Art Gallery, New Haven, Conn., Mabel Brady Garvan Collection

These superb craftsmen executed stylish French-inspired chests, bureaus, tables, card tables, dressing tables and chairs in solid mahogany. Popular at the same time, especially in New England in the shops of John and Thomas Seymour, were elaborate case pieces using fine satinwood and mahogany veneers and inlays as their predominant features. Many of Adam's decorative designs, such as swags, garlands and classical urns, were used by carvers who gave their work a three-dimensional quality and by craftsmen who executed them in delicately shaded inlay.

American country furniture throughout the seventeenth and eighteenth centuries tended to be similar in design to fine city pieces, but there were exceptions. Whenever European settlers established themselves in the same region in America, they continued to use European forms and decorations as well. The painted chest (plate 98) is typical of the pieces created by the Germans in Pennsylvania during the eighteenth and the first half of the nineteenth century.

The Windsor chair was used in the early eighteenth century in England as a garden seat or a piece of porch furniture. In America, where Windsors (plate 99) were first introduced in Pennsylvania during the mid-eighteenth century, they shared space in the finest parlors with elegant mahogany pieces. They were soon adopted by people living in rural areas, and they continue to be made even today.

98

As networks of new roads and canals were built during the closing years of the eighteenth century, communication and transportation became faster and easier. Under such circumstances the country cabinet-maker was made aware of city fashions more quickly. By the time the mass production of furniture became a realistic possibility in the 1830s and 1840s, the gradations of style from city to country had all but disappeared.

99

7   Advice for the Collector

Collecting furniture can be not only an enjoyable but a worthwhile hobby, for well-constructed pieces from the past are an investment in the future.

Building a collection of furniture is no different from building a collection of other works of art. Those who develop in-depth knowledge will inevitably search out the finest pieces.

There are many ways of acquiring expertise: visiting museums, subscribing to trade magazines, studying authoritative books, attending antiques shows and visiting antiques shops are some of the things one can do.

The collector must of course learn to distinguish reproductions from authentic antiques. It is important to remember that furniture is always dated by its latest feature; some authentic pieces actually have design elements from several successive periods. When a piece incorporates a combination of styles, however, it is often a reproduction or a revival example. These are of substantially less value than the earlier period pieces they are seeking to emulate.

The ability to interpret signs of wear is important. Remember, wear always occurs in the obvious places—exactly where you would expect it. Because a chair is often dragged across the floor, the bottoms of the legs or feet are covered with tiny "use scratches" and are discolored. In addition to the wear on the feet, wear occurs on the arms, on the seat frame, on the back and on the stretchers. One quite accurate way of testing a chair is to approach it from the back, pick it up and move it across the room. Chances are very good that others have put their hands in exactly the same places when moving the piece. An old chair will almost inevitably show discoloration of the finish in these spots. Over an extended period of time, wood acquires a *patina* (the surface appearance of an aged object) that is difficult to simulate. It is always wise to scrutinize the finials on the tops of the back posts. Like the feet, they are vulnerable parts of the piece and frequently break off and have to be repaired. If finials fail to show signs of wear or their color is different from that of the rest of the piece, check the piece carefully.

Tables are often given a new top when the original wears out. Turn a table upside down and check to see whether the underside of the top and the underside of the leaves match in color. If the piece is a gateleg, swing the leg to see if there is a rub mark where it moves against the underside of the leaf.

The collector must also learn to recognize restoration, since it is a factor that greatly affects the market value of a piece. Highboys, secretaries and other case pieces constructed in two parts are especially tricky. Sometimes the top portion of a highboy becomes separated from the bottom. Dealers attempt to "marry" the top of one piece to the bottom of another. This "marriage" can be disguised by applying new moldings at the joinings. A married piece may have historical interest but a limited monetary value. Regardless of how beautiful it might be or how skillfully the two parts have been joined, it will never represent a worthwhile investment.

Through the years many chairs have lost their feet. A competent restorer can "end off" or replace them. If the signs of wear mentioned earlier are not visible, there is a good possibility that the feet have been replaced. A chair to which this has been done is substantially less interesting to a collector than one that is completely original.

Purchasing furniture that has been completely reupholstered is asking for trouble. It is best to see pieces before the upholstery has been applied, but if this is not possible, the collector should acquire reupholstered pieces only from very reputable, reliable dealers and demand a written guarantee.

The ability to distinguish differences between various kinds of wood should be developed, for this skill will help you determine the country in which a piece was constructed. The bodies of many case pieces were fashioned from fine-quality woods, whereas *secondary woods* (woods of lesser quality) were used for drawer linings and other concealed elements. Furniture from different countries and from different geographic areas within those countries is often easily identified by the secondary woods used in construction. If you are confused about woods, there is a foolproof manner by which they can be identified—the microanalysis that is available through many museums.

When considering the acquisition of a major piece of furniture, always protect yourself by demanding a written guarantee. Any reputable dealer will gladly provide such a document, which should include a description of the piece, the date of its construction, notation of all restoration and a signed statement indicating that your money will be refunded if the piece should vary from the description on the guarantee.

Remember that the only happy collector is an informed one.

Glossary

apron, the horizontal piece of wood below a tabletop, chair seat, looking glass or underframing of a case piece; also called a skirt.

backstool, an early term for a chair without arms.

ball foot, a round, turned foot used chiefly on furniture of the seventeenth and early eighteenth centuries.

baluster, an upright support, usually turned and often topped by a rail. It is also called a banister.

bergère, a French term for an upholstered chair, with closed arms and a loose seat cushion.

Bible box, a carved wooden box with a hinged, sometimes sloping, lid. It was a repository for books or writing materials.

block front, the front of a case piece carved in three parts with the center section either extended beyond or recessed behind the side sections.

bodice back, an upholstered chair back suggestive of the shape of a woman's bodice.

bombé, descriptive of furniture that has rounded, convex or bulging fronts and sides; literally, "blown out."

boss, a knoblike, projecting ornament, usually found on chests.

breakfront, a case piece with a central section that projects beyond the end sections.

broken pediment, a triangular or curved pediment deliberately interrupted at its highest point.

bun foot, a slightly flattened, round foot.

burl, a protruding, irregularly grained growth on a tree. It is often used in thinly sliced sections as veneer.

cabriole leg, a reverse-curved leg ending in a shaped foot.

cartouche, an ornamental device in the form of an unrolled scroll or an oval tablet with the edges scrolled or rolled over.

case piece, a piece of furniture intended to contain something.

chinoiserie, Western style of decoration in imitation of Chinese decoration.

cipher, a monogram; intertwined initials.

classical order, the formal arrangement of columns or pilasters, including their base moldings and capitals and their entablatures, as developed in ancient Greece and Rome and revived during the Renaissance.

claw-and-ball foot, a carved foot resembling a claw holding a ball.

commode, a low chest of drawers, or a cabinet on legs.

console table, a side table usually without back legs. The top is supported by one or more brackets, or consoles; often fixed to the wall.

court cupboard, a rectangular cupboard, either with three tiers of open shelves, or with open top and bottom shelves and an enclosed, recessed cabinet on the middle tier.

crest rail, the top rail of a chair, settee or any other seating form.

C-scroll, a scroll carved in the form of the letter C.

cup turning, a turning resembling an upside-down cup or bowl.

curule chair, a chair with a cross-base support.

cushioned pad foot, a *pad foot* resting upon a disk.

dished top, a tabletop that has been hollowed out of a thick plank of wood, with the resulting dish-shaped surface.

dovetail, a right-angled joint formed by interlacing tenons resembling the shape of a dove's tail.

dowel, a wooden pin or peg used to join two pieces of wood.

emboss, to raise a surface in relief.

fall front, the writing board of a desk, which falls forward to form the writing surface.

finial, a terminal ornament.

fretwork, a design resembling latticework.

gadroon, fluting or reeding ornamentation, often in a spiral design.

gallery, open fretwork or a small balustrade forming a railing around the top of a piece of furniture.

gateleg table, a drop-leaf table with stretcher-connected legs that form a swinging gate to support the leaves.

gesso, a preparation of plaster of Paris and glue used to make a surface for painting.

gilt, a thin layer of gold or something simulating it.

highboy, a tall chest of drawers, usually in two sections: an upper case with drawers and a tall-legged lower case, also with drawers; the upper case rests upon the lower case. Originally known as a high chest.

inlay, decoration formed by contrasting materials set into the surface of a piece.

japanned decoration, simulated Oriental lacquering by the use of varnish or paint with decoration in low relief, usually in chinoiserie designs.

joinery, a technique of joining fitted pieces without nails or pegs.

kneehole, the open space in the center front of a desk or chest of drawers, flanked by a row of drawers on each side.

lacquer, spirit varnish applied in many layers on a wood surface to build up a hard, highly polished surface.

linenfold, a decoration of paneling that resembles folded linen.

lowboy, a low chest or dressing table with drawers, often matching a highboy.

marquetry, inlay of thinly sliced materials such as wood, ivory, bone, metal or mother-of-pearl into a background of veneer.

monopodium, a support derived from an ancient design, consisting of an animal leg surmounted by an animal head.

mortise-and-tenon, the method of joining two pieces of wood by inserting a tenon, or extension, of one piece into the mortise, or socket, of another.

pad foot, the simple flattish end of a cabriole leg.

papeleira, a *vargueño* without a fall front.

parquetry, veneering in abstract geometric patterns.

patina, color and texture of a surface produced by age and wear.

Pembroke table, a small, rectangular, drop-leaf table, usually with straight legs.

pier glass, a mirror designed to hang on the section of a wall between two windows or doors.

press cupboard, a cupboard with both the lower and upper sections containing drawers or storage space with doors.

reeding, a semicircular relief motif resembling straight, stylized reeds.

relief, raised ornament or sculpture.

secondary woods, inexpensive and/or imperfect woods used for drawer linings, backs and carcasses of case pieces and other structural elements not readily visible.

secretary, a desk, usually slant-top, with a bookcase above.

settee, a seat with back and arms large enough for two.

settle, a long seat with a high or low closed back, and solid wood ends.

sideboard, a long cabinet for holding dishes of food and usually having drawers and shelves for linens and silver.

slipper foot, a long, slender, pointed foot.

spade foot, a foot somewhat wider than the leg, in profile similar to the shape of a spade.

spindle, a thin turned member.

splat, the vertical center support in a chair back.

S-scroll, a scroll in the form of the letter S.

stiles, the vertical side supports of a chair back.

strapwork, flat, interlaced bands applied or carved on a surface.

stretchers, crosspieces or rungs connecting the legs of chairs, tables, settees, etc.

tester, the wooden or fabric canopy of a high-post bed.

tilt-top table, a table with a top that can be tipped to a vertical position.

trifid foot, a three-toed foot.

trumpet turning, a turning with the profile of a flaring trumpet turned upward.

turning, a way of forming columnar-shaped members of chairs, tables and cupboards by means of a revolving lathe.

vargueño, a Spanish fall-front cabinet supported on a trestle stand or on a cupboardlike base.

veneer, a thin layer of decorative material glued to a thicker backing.

verre églomisé, glass painted on the reverse used as decorative inserts on furniture.

volute, a spiral scroll.

whorl foot, a foot in the shape of an upturned scroll.

Reading and Reference

General and International

APRÀ, NIETTA. *The Louis Styles: Louis XIV, Louis XV, Louis XVI.* New York: World Publishing, 1973.

ARONSON, JOSEPH. *The Encyclopedia of Furniture.* 3d ed., rev. New York: Crown Publishers, 1965.

GLOAG, JOHN. *A Social History of Furniture Design: From B.C. 1300 to A.D. 1960.* New York: Crown Publishers, 1966.

HALE, WILLIAM HARLAN, ED. *The Horizon Book of Ancient Greece.* New York: American Heritage Publishing Co., 1965.

HAYWARD, HELENA, ED. *World Furniture.* New York: McGraw-Hill Book Co., 1965.

MERCER, ERIC. *Furniture 700–1700.* New York: Meredith Press, 1969.

PAYNE, ROBERT, ED. *The Horizon Book of Ancient Rome.* New York: American Heritage Publishing Co., 1966.

American

BISHOP, ROBERT. *Centuries and Styles of the American Chair 1640–1970.* New York: E. P. Dutton and Co., 1972.

BISHOP, ROBERT. *How to Know American Antique Furniture.* New York: E. P. Dutton and Co., 1973.

BJERKOE, ETHEL H. *The Cabinetmakers of America.* Exton, Penna.: Schiffer Publishing, 1978.

BURROUGHS, PAUL H. *Southern Antiques.* Richmond, Va.: Garrett & Massie, Inc., Publishers, 1931.

COMSTOCK, HELEN, ED. *The Concise Encyclopedia of American Antiques.* New York: Hawthorn Books, 1958.

CORNELIUS, CHARLES O. *Furniture Masterpieces of Duncan Phyfe.* 1922. Reprint. New York: Dover Publications, 1970.

DAVIDSON, MARSHALL B., ED. *The American Heritage History of Colonial Antiques.* New York: American Heritage Publishing Co., 1967.

DOWNS, JOSEPH. *American Furniture, Queen Anne and Chippendale Periods, in the Henry Francis du Pont Winterthur Museum.* New York: Macmillan Co., 1952.

FALES, DEAN A., AND ROBERT BISHOP. *American Painted Furniture 1660–1880.* New York: E. P. Dutton and Co., 1972.

HALSEY, RICHARD T. H., AND CHARLES O. CORNELIUS. *A Handbook of the American Wing.* 7th ed., revised by Joseph Downs. Metropolitan Museum of Art, 1942.

HORNOR, WILLIAM MACPHERSON, JR. *Blue Book, Philadelphia Furniture, William Penn to George Washington, with special reference to the Philadelphia-Chippendale School.* 1935. Reprint. Washington, D.C.: Highland House Publishers, 1977.

KETTELL, RUSSELL H. *The Pine Furniture of Early New England.* 1929. Reprint. New York: Dover Publications, 1956.

LOCKWOOD, LUKE VINCENT. *Colonial Furniture in America.* 2 vols. 1926. Reprint. New York: Charles Scribner's Sons, 1970.

NUTTING, WALLACE. *Furniture of the Pilgrim Century 1620–1720.* 2 vols. New York: Dover Publications, 1965.

English

ADAM, ROBERT, AND JAMES ADAM. *The Architecture, Decoration and Furniture of Robert and James Adam.* Selected from *The Works in Architecture of Robert and James Adam.* 1880. Reprint. London: Robert Martin's Press, 1975.

BELL, J. MUNRO, ED. *The Furniture Designs of Chippendale, Hepplewhite and Sheraton.* New York: Robert M. McBride and Co., 1938.

CHIPPENDALE, THOMAS. *The Gentleman and Cabinet-Maker's Director.* 3d ed. 1762. Reprint. New York: Dover Publications, 1966.

EDWARDS, RALPH. *The Shorter Dictionary of English Furniture.* New York: Hamlyn/American, 1976.

FASTNEDGE, RALPH W. *English Furniture Styles from 1500 to 1830.* Baltimore: Penguin Books, 1964.

HARRIS, EILEEN. *The Furniture of Robert Adam.* New York: St. Martin's Press, 1973.

INCE, WILLIAM, AND JOHN MAYHEW. *The Universal System of Household Furniture.* 1762. Reprint. London: Alec Tiranti, 1960.

JOY, EDWARD T. *The Book of English Furniture.* South Brunswick, N.J.: A. S. Barnes & Co., 1966.

KENWORTHY-BROWNE, J. A. *Chippendale and His Contemporaries.* London: Orbis Publishing, 1975.

Sheraton Furniture Designs: From the Cabinet-Maker and Upholsterer's Drawing Book, 1791–94. Preface by Ralph Edwards. London: J. Tiranti, 1946.

SHERATON, THOMAS. *The Cabinet-Maker and Upholsterer's Drawing Book.* 1791–94. Reprint. New York: Dover Publications, 1977.

STALKER, JOHN, AND GEORGE PARKER. *A Treatise of Japanning and Varnishing.* 1688. Reprint. London: Alec Tiranti, 1971.

STILLMAN, DAMIE. *The Decorative Work of Robert Adam.* New York: St. Martin's Press, 1973.

Some Public Collections of Furniture

UNITED STATES

Boston: Museum of Fine Arts
Chicago: The Art Institute of Chicago
Cleveland: Cleveland Museum of Art
Dearborn, Mich.: Greenfield Village and Henry Ford Museum
Detroit: The Detroit Institute of Arts
Malibu, Cal.: J. Paul Getty Museum
Milwaukee: Milwaukee Public Museum
Minneapolis: The Minneapolis Institute of Arts
Newark, N. J.: The Newark Museum
New Haven, Conn.: Yale University Art Gallery
New York City: Cooper-Hewitt Museum, the Smithsonian Institution's
  National Museum of Design
  The Frick Collection
  The Metropolitan Museum of Art
Philadelphia: Philadelphia Museum of Art
  The University Museum
Richmond: Virginia Museum of Fine Arts
San Francisco: M. H. de Young Memorial Museum
Toledo, Ohio: The Toledo Museum of Art
Washington, D. C.: Smithsonian Institution
  National Museum of History and Technology
Williamsburg, Va.: Colonial Williamsburg
Winterthur, Del.: The Henry Francis du Pont Winterthur Museum

OTHER

Amsterdam: Rijksmuseum
Bath, England: The American Museum in Britain
Berlin: Kunstgewerbemuseum
Cairo: The Egyptian Museum
Copenhagen: Rosenborg Castle
Florence: Palazzo Pitti
  Palazzo Vecchio/Palazzo della Signoria
Fontainebleau: Musée National du Château de Fontainebleau
London: British Museum
  Victoria and Albert Museum
  Wallace Collection
Munich: Bayerisches Nationalmuseum
  Residenzmuseum
Newcastle-upon-Tyne, England: Laing Art Gallery and Museum
Paris: Musée de Cluny
  Musée des Arts Décoratifs
  Musée du Louvre
Venice: Ca' Rezzonico
Versailles: Musée National du Château de Versailles et des Trianons
Vienna: Österreichisches Museum für angewandte Kunst

Index

Numbers in *italics* indicate pages on which black-and-white illustrations appear.
Numbers in **boldface** indicate pages on which colorplates appear.

A

Adam, Robert, 112, *112*, **113**, 118
Aesop's Fables, scene from, *114*
Alberti, Leon Battista, 35
American furniture, *10*, *11*, 59, 63, 73, 75–83, *75*, *76*, *77*, **78**, *79*, *80*, *81*, *82*, *114*, 115–19, *115*, *116*, *117*, *118*, *119*. See also Baltimore, Boston, Charleston, Connecticut, Massachusetts, New England, Newport, New York City, New York State, Pennsylvania, Philadelphia *and* Williamsburg furniture
Ashur-bani-pal, 18, *18*
Assyrian furniture, 17–18, *18*
Avril, Étienne, **95**

B

Baltimore furniture, *116*, 117
Bartermann, J., 59
Baumhauer, Joseph, *92*
bed-chair, Dutch, baroque, 58–59
beds: American, colonial, 77; Byzantine, 24–25; Carolingian, 27–28; Egyptian, 14, *16* (headrest for), 17; English, Renaissance, 46; French, rococo, 94; Gothic, 30; Greek, 19–20, *20*; Italian, Gothic, 33, Renaissance, 35, *39*, 46, baroque-rococo, **102**; Roman, 21
benches: American, colonial, 77; Byzantine, 24; Carolingian, 27; Egyptian, 14; Etruscan, 21; Flemish, Gothic, **26–27**, 32; French, baroque, 51; Greek, 18; prehistoric, 13
Beneman, Jean-Guillaume, 97
bergère: 90, *90*, 91; *en commodité*, 91; *en confessional*, 91
birdcage, English, Gothic style, *111*
block-and-shell carving, *10*, *114*, *115*, 117
block front, *10*, *80*, *81*, *114*, *115*
bombé, 84, *86*, *92*, **93**, *99*
bonheur-du-jour, 88
bookcases: American, Chippendale, *114*, 115, *115*; English, Gothic style, *111*, William and Mary, 71
Boston furniture, 79, 83, 115, 117
Boucher, François, 88
Boulle, André-Charles, 51–53, **52**, 69
Brustolon, Andrea, *54*, *103*
buffet-cabinet, Netherlandish, Renaissance, *42*, 43
bureau (desk): *à cylindre*, 90, 91; *du Roi Louis XV*, 90; *en pente*, 91; *en tombeau*, 91; *plat*, 91
bureau-cabinets: English, baroque, **74**; German, rococo, 97, *97*
Byzantine furniture, 24–25

C

Cabinet and Chair-Maker's Real Friend and Companion, The (Manwaring), 112
Cabinet-Maker and Upholsterer's Drawing Book, The (Sheraton), 112
Cabinet-Maker and Upholsterer's Guide, The (Hepplewhite), 112
cabinet-on-stand: English, baroque, *64*, *65*, 67; Flemish, baroque, **6**; Italian, baroque, 48, *54*, *55*, 56
cabinets: Dutch, baroque, 56, 58, rococo, 99; French, baroque, *54*, Renaissance, 46; German, baroque, 58, Renaissance, 41, *42*; Indian, lacquer, 66; Italian, baroque, 53, baroque-rococo, *101*; Oriental, lacquer, 65–66
cabriole legs, *11*, 56, 58–59, 68, 71, 73, 79, *82*, 84, 112
Campin, Robert, **26–27**
candlestands, English, baroque-rococo, *106*
Carlin, Jean-Henri Martin, 97
Carolingian furniture, 27–28
cassone (chest), 35–36, *36*, **37**, *38*
cathedra (Roman chair), 22, *23*, 24
chairs: American, bodice-back, *82*, 83, chair-table, 76, Chippendale, *11*, *114*, colonial, 77, easy, 79, neoclassical, 118, Queen Anne, 79, *82*, 83, tall cane-backed, 79, Windsor, 118, *119*; Assyrian, 18, *18*; Byzantine, 24; Dutch East Indian, burgomaster's swivel, made for export, *58*; Egyptian, *12*, 14, 17; English, baroque, 68, 69, Chinese style, *111*, 18th cent., 112, 115, medallion-back, *112*, Queen Anne, **72**, 73, reading, or cockfighting, 71, Regency, 115, Renaissance, 46, turned, 59, 63, William and Mary, 68, 69, Windsor, 118; Etruscan, *20*, 21; French, baroque, 50, 51, Renaissance, 46, *46*, rococo, 87, 88, *90*, 91; German, baroque, *63*; German or Swiss, peasant type, *63*; Gothic, 30–31; Greek, 18–19, *19*, 21; Italian, baroque, 53, *54*, baroque-rococo, *100*, Renaissance, 40, *40*, *41*, Venetian lacquer, *104*; Mexican, baroque, 58, *63*; Netherlandish, baroque, 56, Renaissance, 43; Roman, 21, 22, *23*, 25; Spanish, Renaissance, 46
chair-table, American, 76
chaise longue, 91
Charleston (S.C.) furniture, 79, 83
chauffeuse, 91
chest of drawers: American, Chippendale, 115, colonial, 77; English, baroque, 69. *See also* commodes
chest-on-frame. *See* highboys
chests: American, colonial, 77, dower, 118, *118*, neoclassical, 118; Byzantine, 24; Carolingian, 28; Dutch, baroque, 58; Egyptian, 14, **15**, 17; English, baroque, 68, Renaissance, 46; French, bombé, 84, *86*, *92*, **93**,

Etruscan style, jewel, *96*; German, baroque, 58, **61**; Gothic, 29–30, 31; Greek, 20–21; Italian (*cassoni*), 33, 35–36, *36*, **37**, *38*; Netherlandish, Renaissance, 43; Roman, 21, 23; Romanesque, 28; Spanish, 31
chiffonnière, rococo, 87, 91
chinoiserie, 53, 56, 66, 71, **78**, 79, *105*
Chippendale style, American: highboy, *114*; secretary-bookcase, *114*, *115*; secretary-desk, *10;* side chair, *11*, *114*
Chippendale, Thomas, *107*, 108–12, *108*, **109**, *110*, *111*, 115
City and Country Builder's and Workman's Treasury of Designs (Langley), 108
claw-and-ball foot, *11*, 73, *114*, 115
coiffeuse, 91
Colbert, Jean-Baptiste, 49–51
commodes: French, baroque, **52**, 53, rococo, *86*, *92*, **93**, *94*; German, rococo, 97, *98*; Italian, Venetian lacquer, *105*
Connecticut furniture, *76*, 117
Corradini, Antonio, *100*
couches: Assyrian, 18, *18*; Egyptian, 14, 17; Etruscan, 21; French, rococo, 91; Greek, 19–20, *20*, 22; Roman, 22, *22*, 25
country furniture, American, 118–19, *118*, *119*
courant, 91
cradles, 36, *39*, 40
credenza, 40
Cresson, L., *90*
C-scrolls, 66, **67**, 79, 84
Cucci, Domenico, 51
cupboards: American, colonial, 77, linen press, *80*, press, *76*; Byzantine, 25; Dutch, baroque, 56, 58, rococo, *101*; English, baroque, 68, court, 46, *47*, *64*; Flemish, plate, **32**; French, Renaissance, **34**, *44*, *45*, rococo, *95*; German, baroque, 58, Renaissance, 41, *42*; Gothic, plate, 31, *33*; Greek, 21; Roman, 22–23
curule, 115
Cuvilliés, François, 97

D

Datini, Francesco, 36
daybeds: American, baroque, 79; English, baroque, 69, *69*, 73, Regency, 115; French, rococo, 91
Dennis, Thomas, 76
desks: American, Chippendale, *10*, colonial, 79; Carolingian, 28; English, baroque, 68, 71, Gothic, 28, *29*; French, rococo, 90, 91; Spanish, baroque, 46, 58, *60*, **61**
Diderot's *Encyclopédie*, plates from, *endpapers*, 87
diphros (X stool), 18, *19*
Director (Chippendale). See *Gentleman and Cabinet-Maker's Director, The*

Du Cerceau, Jacques-Androuet, **34**, 43, *45*
Duplessis, Jean-Claude, *90*
Dutch East India Company, 56
Dutch furniture, 56, 58, *58–59*, 59, 69, 81, 83, 97, *99. See also* Netherlandish furniture
Duyckinck, Gerardus, 83

E
ébénistes, 88
Egyptian furniture, **12**, 13–17, *14*, **15**, *16*, 20, 29, 31
English East India Company, 65, 73
English furniture, *29*, 30, 46, 47, 59, 63, 64–74, *64*, *65*, **67**, 68, 69, 70, 71, *72*, **74**, 75, 77, 79, 83, *106*, *107*, 108–12, *108*, **109**, *110*, *111*, *112*, **113**, 115
Etruscan furniture, 20, 21, *21*
Etruscan style, 94, *96*

F
firescreen, English, rococo, **109**
Fitzhugh, William, 77
Flemish furniture, **6**, **26–27**, **32**. *See also* Netherlandish furniture
Flötner, Peter, 41
Foggini, G. B., *55*
folding chairs: Gothic, 30; Italian, Renaissance, 40
folding stools: Carolingian, 27; Egyptian, 17; Greek, 18; Roman, 22, 24, *25*; Romanesque, 28
Fontaine, Pierre-F.-L., 115
footstools or footrests: Assyrian, 18, *18*; Egyptian, 14; French, rococo, 88; Greek, 18
French furniture, *endpapers*, **frontis.**, *28*, 30, 33, *34*, 43–46, *44*, *45*, *46*, 49–53, *50*, *51*, **52**, *54*, 56, 83, 84, 86–97, *86*, *87*, **89**, *90*, *92*, **93**, *95*, *96*, 115, 117

G
Gaudreaux, Antoine, *86*
Gentleman and Cabinet-Maker's Director, The (Chippendale), *107*, *108*, **109**, *110*, *111*, *112*, 115
George I style, 73, **74**
George II style, 108
German furniture, 30, 40–42, 58–59, **61**, *63*, 97, *97*, *98*
Gibbs, James, 70
Goddard, John, 81, 115
Goddard-Townsend school of cabinetmaking. *See* Townsend-Goddard dynasty
Goodison, Benjamin, *106*
Gothic style, *111*
Greek furniture, 18–21, *19*, *20*, 22, 27, *36*, 40
guéridon, 91
guilds: English coffer makers', 43; French, 50, 88; 13th cent., 29; 17th cent., 8

H
harpsichord and stool, Italian, baroque, **57**
Hartshorne, Ebenezer, *80*
Hepplewhite, Alice, 112
Hepplewhite, George, 112, 117
Hepplewhite style, American, card table, *116*
highboys: American, Chippendale, *114*, 115; colonial, 79, Queen Anne, 79, *79*, William and Mary, 76, **78**; English, Queen Anne, 79, William and Mary, 69; European, baroque, 115

I
Ince, William, 112
Italian furniture, 21, 30, 33, 35–40, *36*, **37**, *38*, *39*, *40*, *41*, 46, **48**, 53–57, *54*, *55*, **57**, **85**, *100*, 101–5, *101*, **102**, *103*, *104*, *105*

J
japanning, *64*, 66, 68, **78**, 83
Johnson, Edward, 75

K
kases (wardrobes), 43
Kent, William, **72**, 73, **74**, *106*, 108
kettle stand, American, 115
kline (couch), 20, *20*, 24
klismos (chair), 18–19, *19*, 22, 115

L
lacquerwork: Chinese, 65, **93**, 94; French, 94; German, 97; Indian, 66; Oriental, 53, 65–66; Venetian, 103, *104*, 105, *105*; *vernis martin*, 94. *See also* japanning
Langley, Batty and Thomas, 108
Lannuier, Charles-Honoré, 117, *117*
Le Brun, Charles, 49–51
Lépine, Jean-Antoine, *90*
Le Vau, Louis, 53
linen press, American, Queen Anne, *80*
Linnell, John, **113**
Lock, Matthias, *107*, 108
looking glasses, French, baroque, 51, rococo, 88
looking-glass frames: American, baroque, 83; English, rococo, *107*
Louis XIV, or French baroque, style, 49–53, 83, 94; armchair, *50*; commode, **52**; *torchère*, *51*
Louis XV, or rococo, style, **frontis.**, 84, 86–94, *86*, *87*, **89**, *90*, *92*, **93**
Louis XVI, or neoclassical, style, 94, **95**, *96*
lowboys: American, Chippendale, 115, colonial, 79, Queen Anne, 79, *81*; English, William and Mary, 69, *71*
Low Countries. *See* Dutch furniture, Flemish furniture *and* Netherlandish furniture

M
Macé, Jean, 53, *54*
Manufacture Royale des Glaces à Miroir (Paris), 51
Manufacture Royale des Meubles de la Couronne (Paris), 50
Manwaring, Robert, 112
Marie Antoinette, 94, 97
Marot, Daniel, 71, 73
marquetry, **6**, 9, 56, 58, **61**, *67*, 68, 88, *90*, *92*, 94, 97, *98*, 112
Massachusetts furniture, 76, *78*, *80*, 115, *116*, 117, *119*
Mayhew, John, 112
McIntire, Samuel, *116*
Meissonnier, Juste-Aurèle, 83
menuisiers, 88
Merode Altarpiece, **26–27**
meublant, 91
Mexican furniture, 58, *63*
Michelozzo di Bartolommeo, 35
mirrors: *See* looking glasses, looking-glass frames *and* pier glasses
Misson, Maximilian, 103
Mitnacht, Hieronymous, 59

N
Netherlandish furniture, 30, 33, 42–43, *42*, 56. *See also* Dutch furniture *and* Flemish furniture
New England furniture, *11*, 75, *75*, 77, 79
Newport (R.I.) furniture, *10*, 79, 81, *81*, *114*, 115
New York City furniture, 79, 83, 115, 117–18, *117*
New York State furniture, 76, 79, 81, *82*, 83

O
Oeben, Jean-François, *90*
Onofri, Crescenzio, **57**
organ case, English, rococo, *110*

P
Palazzo Farnese (Rome), table from, *39*
papeleira (writing box), 46, 58, *60*
Parker, George, 66
parquetry, 9, 69, 94
Passe, Crispyn de, 43
pedestals: English, 18th cent., 112, **113**; French, baroque, *51*
Pembroke table, American, 115
Pennsylvania furniture, 118, *118*
Percier, Charles, 115
Philadelphia furniture, *11*, 79, *82*, 83, *114*, 115, 117
Phyfe, Duncan, 117
pier glasses, English, baroque-rococo, *106*, *107*
Piffetti, Pietro, 103
Pineau, Nicolas, **frontis.**, *84*
Piranesi, Giovanni Battista, 112
Pompadour, Madame de, *84*, 88, 94
Pompeiian style. *See* Etruscan style
poudreuse, 91
prehistoric furniture, 7–8, 13

Q
Queen Anne style, American: 79–83, 115; bodice-back chairs, *82*, 83; highboy, *79*; linen press, *80*; lowboy, *81*; settee, *82*
Queen Anne style, English: 73; room of furniture, *70*; side chairs, **72**

R
Recueil de décorations intérieures (Percier and Fontaine), 115
Régence period, 83, *84*, 91
Regency style, English, 115
Riesener, Jean-Henri, *90*, 97
Roentgen, Abraham, 97, *98*
Roentgen, David, 97
Romanesque furniture, 28, *29*
Roman furniture, 21–24, *22*, *23*, *25*, 27, 31, *36*, *38*

S
Sambin, Hugues, **34**, 43, *45*, 46
Savonarola chair, *40*
Schnell, Martin, 97
Schwerdfeger, Jean-Ferdinand, *96*
secrétaire, 91
secretary-bookcase, American, Chippendale, *114*, 115
secretary-desk, American, Chippendale, *10*
sedan chair, Italian, rococo, **85**
serpentine form, 81, *81*, 84, *86*, *98*, 115
servant, 91

settees: American, Queen Anne, *82*; English, Queen Anne, 73
settles: American, colonial, 77; Flemish, Gothic, **26–27**; French, Gothic, *28*; Gothic, 31
Sèvres porcelain, *87*, 88, 91, **95**, *96*
Seymour, John and Thomas, 118
sgabello chair, *40*
Shaw, Henry, *33*
Sheraton style, American, side table, *116*
Sheraton, Thomas, 112, 115, 117
showcase on stand, Italian, baroque, **48**
sideboard, *40*, 112
sideboard suite, English, 18th cent., **113**
sofas: American, Chippendale, 115; French, rococo, 88
Spanish Colonial furniture (Mexican), 58, *63*
Spanish furniture, 31, 33, 46, 56, 58, *60*, **61**, *62*
Specimens of Ancient Furniture (Shaw), *33*
S-scrolls, 66, 79, 84
Stalker, John, 66
stollenschrank (buffet-sideboard), 40
stools: Byzantine, 24; Carolingian, 27; Egyptian, 14, *14*, 17, 31; English, Renaissance, 46, William and Mary, **67**; French, rococo, 88; Gothic, 31; Greek, 18, *19*, 21; Italian, baroque, **57**; prehistoric, 13; Roman, 22, 31. *See also* folding stools *and* footstools
Strohmeier, Lienhart, 41

T
table à la tronchin, 91
table de nuit, 91
tables: American, butterfly, 79, card, 79, *117*, chair-table, *76*, colonial, 77, gateleg, *11*, 77, Hepplewhite, *116*, mixing, 79, neoclassical, 118, Pembroke, 115, Queen Anne, 79, Sheraton, *116*, splay-legged, 79, tea, 79, trestle, 75, William and Mary, 77; Assyrian, *18*, *18*; Byzantine, 24, *25*; Carolingian, 27; Dutch, baroque, 58; Egyptian, 14, *14*, 16, 17, 20; English, baroque-rococo, *107*, Regency, 115, Renaissance, 46, sideboard, **113**; Flemish, Gothic, **26–27**; French, baroque, *51*, Gothic, *28*, Renaissance, 46, rococo, *86*, *87*, 88, **89**, 91; German, baroque, 58, Renaissance, 41, rococo, *98*; Gothic, 30; Greek, 20; Italian, baroque, 53, Renaissance, *39*, 40, rococo, *103*; Netherlandish, baroque, 56; Roman, 22; Spanish, baroque, 58, *62*
Ten Books of Architecture (Alberti), 35
tête-à-tête (also called *causeuse, confidante, marquise*), 91
Thomire, Pierre-Philippe, *96*
thrones: Assyrian, *18*; Byzantine, 24; Egyptian, 14; Flemish, Gothic, **32**; French, Gothic, *28*, Louis XIV's, 51; German, baroque, *63*; Greek, 18, 21; Italian, baroque-rococo, *100*; Roman, 22
thymiaterion (lamp holder), 21
Tilliard, Jean-Baptiste, *90*
torchère, 51
Townsend-Goddard dynasty, 79, *114*
Townsend, Job, 79, *81*, 115
Treatise of Japanning and Varnishing, A (Stalker and Parker), 66, 79, 83
Tutankhamun, furniture from tomb of, 17; ceremonial chair, **12**; chest, **15**; headrest, *16*

U
Universal System of Household Furniture, The (Ince and Mayhew), 112
upholsterers at work, French, 18th cent., *endpapers*, 87

V
Vandercruse, Roger, *87*
Vanrisamburgh, Bernard II, 88, *89*, **89**, 91
vargueño (writing box), 46, 58, **61**
verre églomisé, **72**
Versailles, 51, 52, 53, 84, 97
videpoche, 91
Vignola, Giacomo da, *39*
voyeuse, *90*, 91
Vredeman de Vries, Hans, 43

W
wardrobes: English, rococo, *108*; French, baroque, 53; German, Renaissance, 41; Gothic, 31; Netherlandish, Renaissance, 43; Spanish, Gothic, 31, 33
Weisweiler, Adam, 97
William and Mary style, American, 79; gateleg table, 77; highboys, *76*, **78**
William and Mary style, English, 69, 71, 73; daybed, *69*; side chairs, *68*; stool, **67**; wing chair, *68*
Williamsburg (Va.) furniture, 79, 83
Windsor chairs: American, 118, *119*; English, 118
Wood, William, 75

Acknowledgments

Cooper-Hewitt staff members have been responsible for the following contributions to the series: concept, Lisa Taylor; administration, John Dobkin and Christian Rohlfing; coordination, Pamela Theodoredis. In addition, valuable help has been provided by S. Dillon Ripley, Joseph Bonsignore, Susan Hamilton and Robert W. Mason of the Smithsonian Institution, as well as by the late Warren Lynch, Gloria Norris and Edward E. Fitzgerald of Book-of-the-Month Club, Inc.

The authors wish to thank the following for their kind assistance: Anne Cohen De Pietro, Brenda Gilchrist, Lisa Little, David McFadden, Christian Rohlfing and Lisa Taylor—and extend a special thank you to Joan Hoffman for her skillful editing of the text.

Credits